CROAT
for
TRAVELERS

-The total guide-

The comprehensive traveling guide for all your traveling needs.

PUBLISHED BY

TABLE OF CONTENTS

Chapter 1: Welcome to Croatia, the perfect year-round destination

Croatia is known to be one of the most interesting countries around the globe. This country offers so many places I'm sure you will love visiting and activities you'll love experiencing.

Located in between Central Europe, Southeast Europe, and the Mediterranean, Croatia truly has something for everyone. It is a lush, modern country, which meanders over picturesque bays, forests, and hills.

Croatia shares borders with Hungary to the northeast, Serbia to the east, Bosnia and Herzegovina to the southeast, Montenegro to the southeast, and Slovenia to the northwest. The country covers 56,594 square kilometers, and the distances between cities are easy to underemphasize.

Croatia is not overpopulated and offers a friendly, laid-back atmosphere that is popular with travellers who tend to regard it as a favored holiday destination. With more than 1100 islands in the Adriatic Sea, it is hardly a surprise that travellers of all ages and interests regularly choose to book vacations in Croatia, and the country constantly ranks as one of the world's best holiday destinations. Finally, Croatia is one of the most popular holiday destinations of this century, and before you have even left, you will want to come back. Dive into these chapters, and you will understand why.

Chapter 2: A concise history of Croatia

Croatia's history is an inexhaustible topic. Numerous books have been written on individual kings, dukes, rulers, and historical eras. Paleolithic era is the period of the earliest known occupation of Croatia by humans. Archaeologists have found a plethora of objects made by pre-Neanderthal people, while the remains of Neanderthal humans were found in the region of Zagorje. To delve into this period of the country's past, you can visit the legendary site of the Krapina Neanderthals.

Croatia was later inhabited by Illyrians, and Greek colonies. Thanks to its unique and strategically important position, Croatia was desirable territory for many invaders. As the Romans made their appearance in 9 AD, the area of present-day Croatia fell under the rule of the Roman Empire. Great advances were made in architecture, as evidenced in the Pula Arena, and the Temple of Augustus in Pula. On the other hand, the region of Dalmatia was the birthplace of the Roman Emperor Diocletian, who built a huge Diocletian's Palace in the area known as Split.

The first Croats arrived in the area which is modern-day Croatia in the early 7th century. This period effectively marked the beginning of the Christianization in Croatia. In 879, under duke Branimir, the Pope John VIII recognized our country as an autonomous state. In the following period, Tomislav became the first Croatian king. His exact ancestry is unknown, but he probably originated from the House of Trpimirovic. In 925, Tomislav was crowned at the field of Duvno near Tomislavgrad in modern-day Herzegovina. The medieval Croatian kingdom saw immense social, cultural, and political rise in the 11th century when the Byzantine Dalmatia was annexed to Croatia. The earliest recorded inscription of the Croatian language, the Baška Tablet, dates back to this period.

Stjepan II was the last member of the Trpimirovic dynasty, who had no direct descendants to succeed him. When he passed away, the crown was passed to Ladislaus I of Hungary. Subsequently, the country entered a union with the Kingdom of Hungary in 1102. However, the Republic of Venice gained control over the region of Dalmatia in 1428, and their rule over the southern areas lasted almost four centuries. During this period, the country was under threat from the Ottomans.

As the Turkish invasion eventually progressed, Croatia lost several important territories. The most important events from this period include the Battle of Krbava field and the Battle of Mohacs, both resulting in decisive Turkish victories. In the Battle of Mohacs, the Hungarians were led by King Louis II, while the Turks were led by Suleiman the Magnificent. King Louis II was killed in this battle, which marked the effective destruction of the Hungarian empire. The kingdom of Croatia fell under the rule of the Habsburg Monarchy, while the Turks continued their movement into the Croatian territory until the Battle of Sisak in 1593. This was the first decisive Turkish defeat, as well as one of the most significant victories for the entire Christian world.

The next major event was the Great Turkish War, when Croatia partially regained its lost territories, but Bosnia remained outside our borders. During the 18th century, the Ottomans were driven out of nearly all of Europe.

The early 19th century saw the rise of the Revolutions in Croatia, and the main idea was to unite all South Slavic nations into one state. In 1918, the Croatian Parliament declared independence and decided to join the State of Slovenes, Croats and Serbs, made out of all Southern Slavic nations.

A few decades later, the occupation of Yugoslavia led to some horrible events. The complicated split of Yugoslavia started in 1941, when Germany and Italy occupied the state. Some parts of Croatia, Bosnia and Herzegovina, were merged into the Independent State of Croatia, while parts of Dalmatia were captured by Italy. During this period, the Croatian movement Ustaše was formed. This regime eventually initiated a ruthless program of ethnic cleansing against Serbs.

A later uprising by ethnic Serbs against the Ustaše regime resulted in the creation of the Partisan movement led by Josip Broz Tito. With Allied support, and the assistance of Soviet army, the Partisans gained control of Yugoslavia. In the decades following World War II, Croatia became a Socialist Republic unit of Yugoslavia.

After Tito's death, the political situation in the federation started to go downhill with national tension encouraged by the Serbian Memorandum and the emergence of seizures in Kosovo. And things got even worse when the first multi-party elections were held in our country. Franjo Tuđman won, and he became the first President of Croatia. Soon after, the Serbs proclaimed the autonomy of the Republic of Serbian Krajina, and began the Log Revolution where obstacles were placed across roads throughout the country as a sign of their secession from Croatia.

As time passed, the Croatian parliament declared independence on 25 June 1991. Slovenia declared independence from the federation on the same day. Soon after, tensions turned into the Croatian War of Independence when the YNA and various paramilitary groups attacked Croatia. At that time, Croatia had no regular army. By the end of 1991, thousands of Croats were forced out by the Yugoslav National Army.

The city of Vukovar underwent a total siege, during which most of the city was demolished and a majority of the population was forced to leave. Unfortunately, Vukovar fell to the Serbian forces on 18 November 1991 and the Ovcara massacre occurred. It was the largest massacre and the worst crime committed in Europe since the Second World War.

Several other massacres have also occurred, including the Lovas massacre in Slavonija, and the Erdut massacre. The Škabrnja massacre was unfortunately heavily overshadowed by the happenings in Vukovar. On December 21, 1991 the Serbian Forces attacked the region of Istria. During this horrible period, numerous cities in Croatia were heavily destroyed, including Dubrovnik, Šibenik, Zadar, Vukovar, and Gospi. In order to relieve the siege of these cities, some smaller military operations were undertaken by Croatian forces. In 1992, the country finally gained diplomatic recognition by the United Nations. However, all the diplomatic efforts were useless in bringing security to the region. The Bosnian War against the Serbs began in 1992, as a result of the breakup of Yugoslavia and events in Croatia.

The Croatian War of Independence lasted from 1991 to 1995. On 4 August, Croatia started the legendary Operation Storm. The main goal of this important operation was to recapture the occupied territories in Croatia. The offensive, involving 100,000 lightly armed Croatian men, was the largest single land battle fought on this continent since the Second World War. Operation Storm achieved its main goal and was completed after only four days, on 8 August. This historic battle was also a huge factor in the outcome of the Bosnian War. The Croatian War of Independence finally ended in 1995 with a decisive victory by Croatia and a strategic victory for the Army of the Republic of Bosnia and Herzegovina. Croatia peacefully reintegrated its remaining occupied territories by the end of 1998, and became member of NATO in 2009. In 2013, Croatia joined the European Union.

Chapter 3: Taste of Croatia

Croatian cuisine has developed through centuries of social and political changes, with roots stretching to ancient times. It is noted for its regional diversity, abundance of distinctness in taste, and various forms of cooking. Thanks to its geographical position, Croatia offers a unique fusion of the best of many different regions. Along the pristine coastal regions, the food is Mediterranean, with strong Italian influences. The region of Dalmatia in particular has a wide variety of different ingredients which are commonly used, ranging from fish, vegetables, spices, meats, etc. The basic staples, however, are olive oil, rosemary, oregano, marjoram, lemon, and nutmeg. Pasta dishes and pizza can be found throughout the country. Croatia is blessed with thousands of islands, so our cuisine also features a diverse variety of fish and seafood.

Further inland, in continental Croatia, you can expect to find many Austro-Hungarian dishes, such as goulash. In this part of Croatia, sausages, pork, black pepper, paprika, garlic, potatoes, and various types of cheeses are the most common ingredients. A plate of the famous sheep's milk cheese (paški sir) with fresh tomatoes, olive oil, and air-dried prosciutto (pršut) is the best way to start your meal. Many dishes that were once regional, however, have many different variations throughout the entire country.

Croatian cuisine is also an important part of our culture, social structure and traditions. Traditionally, meals in Croatia generally contain three to four courses. Lunch is typically the main meal of the day, while the quintessential Croatian feast begins with soup, often chicken broth with pasta or semolina dumplings. The main course usually includes meat served with crusty potatoes or rice on the side. Dessert always appears at the table, but it is rarely eaten. After a hearty Croatian lunch, there is no space left for dessert.

Here are some of our most popular traditional dishes. The traditional lamb with different Mediterranean herbs is an essential Croatian cooking type of stew. Janjetina - or lamb - is a very traditional Croatian meal. As a matter of fact, you can find this tasty dish in almost any restaurant or tavern, especially in Dalmatia. This dish is not cheap, but it is worth every penny.

Another very popular dish in Croatia is called Pašticada. It is basically a stewed beef dish, cooked in a tasty sauce, and served with pasta. A scoop of this is enough to understand why it is so celebrated. Accompanied with fresh salad and red wine, this dish will leave you satisfied in every way.

Originating from Zagreb, Zagrebacki Odrezak is the Croatian version of the famous Weiner Schnitzel. This mouth-watering dish has the distinct taste of meat which is accentuated by the accompanying ingredients, and is proudly considered one of Zagreb's most notable and delicious dishes. There are many variations of this dish. However, it is traditionally prepared with veal, filled with ham and cheese and grilled with breadcrumbs.

For many families in Croatia, Sarma is a staple dish, particularly during the holidays. Sarma Cabbage rolls filled with minced pork meat and rice are part of the traditional cuisine of many Central European countries. It definitely doesn't sound like Croatia's most appetizing dish, but it is surprisingly flavorful. Despite its humble ingredients, Sarma is a great main course.

If there is one dessert you must try in Croatia, let it be Zagorski Štrukli. It is a creamy, sticky, dessert made of dough and filled with a mixture of cottage cheese and eggs. Hailing from the region of Hrvatsko Zagorje, it is one of the country's tastiest yet simplest desserts. Because of its rich, briny, tasty flavor, you will want to smuggle some back in your suitcase.

Chapter 4: Seasons in Croatia

Croatia is one of those amazing year-round destinations, with weather that offers something for everyone. But the best months for traveling in Croatia are generally between May and October. August is best avoided as prices increase and popular sights are often too crowded. One week before or after the peak season can make a huge difference in the number of tourists. However, August is a great time to visit Zagreb as the locals go to the coast and hotel prices can significantly drop.

Winters in Zagreb used to be plain and grey. In recent years, however, Advent in Zagreb has become a beautiful time of the year when the entire city is delightfully decorated. A wide array of concerts is also scheduled in the days leading up to Christmas, while the city's Christmas market is a huge draw. In fact, Zagreb was named the Best European Christmas Destination in 2015. It is not hard to see why. This alluring capital has everything you could possibly need to get into the mood of the festive season. Winter temperatures range from -2 to 25°C in the continental region.

In contrast, Croatia's coast and islands, from Istria and Kvarner to Dalmatia enjoy a Mediterranean climate, characterized by prolonged warm and dry summers and cool, rainy winters. During the summer months of June and August, the temperature rises significantly and there are many days when the coast experiences temperatures of over 36°C. Therefore, the summer season is the most heavily tourist trafficked season in Croatia.

Visitors who frequently travel to Croatia know that the best time to visit is during spring, when the temperatures are pretty bearable for walking around (16°C to 21°C). The fall months are also popular, offering pleasant temperatures. This can be a delightful time of year to visit, with beautiful fall foliage and many events that take place throughout the country. Still, the majority of tourists travel to Croatia in the main summer months, although my country is truly magical in every season.

Chapter 5: Zagreb in all its splendor

Zagreb is one of the most popular capital cities in Europe, with its seemingly endless blend of history, culture, splendid attractions, stunning places and affordability. For those living in Europe, this beautiful city is even more of an ideal place to visit, with cheap airfare and flight deals making it both quick and easy to get to.

Zagreb is clearly distinguished by its charming architecture, modern feel, and strong historical background. As the biggest city in Croatia, Zagreb also offers a wealth of attractions, culinary delights, and hidden corners worth exploring. But Zagreb is much more than just a melting pot of cultural wonders.

This quaint capital has always been a special place, and one of those cities in constant transformation. However, Zagreb still retains the everlasting charm of Croatian culture, attracting thousands of tourists every day. The pulsing heart of Croatia, a leader in the cultural, political and economic development of the Balkans, Zagreb is a vibrant metropolitan city with something for everyone. As the capital of Croatia, it is also the seat of the central government. It is a city where there is lots to experience and even more to see and feel.

Situated along the Sava river, at the southern part of the Medvednica mountain, this eclectic city is a magnet for attracting visitors from all over the globe. With a population of almost one million inhabitants, Zagreb can be quite crowded at times. Zagreb is also an important tourist hub, not only in terms of visitors travelling from Western Europe to the Adriatic Sea, but also as a travel destination itself. Since the end of the 1990's, it has attracted close to a million visitors every year. Nevertheless, the city has even bigger potential as many visitors that visit Croatia skip Zagreb in order to visit the beaches along the coast and old historic highlights such as Dubrovnik, Split, and Zadar.

This bustling capital also has a special role in the Republic of Croatia's history, and counts as one of the world's oldest capitals, having nearly 1000 years in age. The earliest known settlement was a Roman Andautonia, now Šćitarjevo in the town of Velika Gorica.

The area that we know as Zagreb today was mentioned for the first time in a document in 1094, when the city was divided into two different sectors: the smaller, Kaptol, inhabited mostly by clergy, and the bigger, Gradec, inhabited mostly by workers. In 1851, these two areas were finally united into Zagreb by Ban Josip Jelacic. Still, the origin of the name Zagreb remains enveloped in the mists of legend. After the country gained its independence, Zagreb was established as its capital.

Getting to & around Zagreb

Zagreb is the biggest international gateway in Croatia, so if you are flying to the country, there is a good chance you will have to visit Zagreb. Zagreb Pleso Airport is the main international airport in the country, and is actually situated in the nearby city called Velika Gorica. The airport is located approximately 15 kilometres from the main railway station in Zagreb. It might seem a daunting task to reach Zagreb, but you will be pleased to know there are several transport options that make travelling into Zagreb city centre much easier than you might have assumed.

At the airport you can rent a car from several car rental companies. For the best deal, it is a good idea to arrange the car hire online. It is also important to note that depending on the time of day, it is likely to take you up to 30 minutes to drive from the airport into Zagreb.

Another option to reach the city center is to catch the airport bus, which will take you to the main bus station in Zagreb. The

16

airport bus can be found right outside the main arrival terminal.

By far, the easiest and most convenient option to reach Zagreb is to take a taxi. Usually, there are a few taxis waiting outside the arrival terminal. The journey normally takes around 20 minutes, depending on your final destination.

Bus, train, tram, you name it, Zagreb has it - public transport in Zagreb is the best and most popular way to get around. Still, I have to admit that Zagreb can be a little bit confusing, especially for a first-time visitor. Let me break this down for you. The area above the square of Ban Jelačić is basically the old section of Zagreb, with the highest concentration of landmarks and points of interest. For amenities that are not within walking distance, take advantage of Zagreb's noteworthy bus network.

The area near the Esplanade Hotel and the main rail station is actually the centre of the city. From here you can reach every other area in Zagreb, including the old section of the city and the Novi Zagreb (New Zagreb). Novi Zagreb is divided into several enormous blocks, and to be completely honest with you, there is nothing particularly interesting to see. However, the Museum of Contemporary Art is definitely worth your attention, as well as one of the biggest shopping centres in the city - Avenue Mall.

If you plan to spend more than a few days in Zagreb, you may want to purchase the Zagreb Card. The Zagreb Card is a must for anyone looking to save money and time while sightseeing. You can either buy a 24-hour card or a 72-hour card. Both cards get you unlimited rides on public transportation, as well as wide range of additional discounts for most of the city's iconic sights and attractions. You can buy the Zagreb Card at the tourist information centre, at any participating location, and also at several hotels and hostels in the city. Check out (http://www.zagrebcard.com) for more details. To get a taxi in Zagreb, simply look for the taxi ranks at the central railway station or around the central square. If you need to call a cab, reliable companies include Taxi Cammeo (1212), and Eko Taxi (060 77 77).

You can easily navigate Zagreb by bus, tram, and on foot, so you may want to explore the city even further. The entire transportation schedule is available on the official web site http://www.zet.hr/. All bus lines and the schedule are also available at bus stops. Daytime trams run every few minutes from 4:00 am to midnight. Night bus services cover the period between 12:00 to 4:00 am. These buses follow the direction of the daytime lines. You can buy your tickets from all bus drivers, however, it is recommended to buy your ticket in advance from a kiosk. Don't forget to validate your paper ticket after boarding the bus or tram. Note that your ticket is valid only for 90 minutes in one direction. Tickets have different prices for daily rides and for night transport.

The best way to explore Zagreb in depth is to take the ever-popular hop-on/hop-off tour. Zagreb currently has two tourist bus lines that offer this kind of service. The red line is 12 km long and runs in the heart of the city, while the green line is 32 km long, and includes places such as Jarun Lake, Bundek Lake, and Maksimir Park. Both tours depart daily between 9 am and 2 pm from Kaptol. You can buy your tickets directly from the driver.

The oldest public transport option though, is the funicular. This isn't the best way of getting around the city as it only operates on a 66m track connecting the Donji Grad to the Gornji Grad. Still, it's a favored tourist attraction that offers a great view of Zagreb.

 Zagreb also features a Tourist Train. It is not really a train but a charming mini vehicle designed to promote tourism in the capital. It operates on a small route in the heart of the city, starting and ending on the central square of Ban Jelacic. It runs every hour from 10 am to 7 pm. And it's absolutely free.

Attractions that make Zagreb so special

Why not start your tour of Zagreb with a stroll around the Old Town or a visit to one of its many museums? Then you can unwind in one of the splendid cafes and bars around the central square of Ban Jelacic, or treat your taste buds to Croatian dishes in one of the Old Town's many tavernas and restaurants. You will be completely amazed by the picturesque flair of this old section, situated at the foot of the famous Ban Jelacic Square. This charming square is located in the heart of the city centre, and is surrounded by a multitude of must-see attractions. The daily Dolac market takes place here too, where you can buy all sorts of tasty food, flowers and fish. The beautiful Manduševac fountain is a well-photographed sight, but the statue of Ban Jelacic in the centre of the square is the focus of much attention.

Apart from the highlights of Zagreb, like the Gornji Grad and Kaptol, St. Mark's Square and the Zagreb Cathedral, you will find yourself enjoying unknown narrow streets, charming cafes, the locals' favorite shopping experience on Ilica Street, the stunning surroundings of the river Sava and the lively park Zrinjevac, featuring street musicians, food stalls, events, and performing shows by the square of King Tomislav (Trg Kralja Tomislava).

Just wander around this area and you will walk by the main rail station in Zagreb, the splendid Esplanade Hotel, increasingly popular Botanical Garden and the beautiful Importanne Center, which perpetually pleases and surprises tourists with a variety of shops, stores, and boutiques.

The old section of the city around the central square is made up of Gornji Grad (Upper Town) and Kaptol, a large medieval urban area packed with churches, narrow streets, museums, galleries and important buildings that are popular attractions. This historic area can be reached on foot, starting from the central square.

Certainly the most famous building on Kaptol is the Zagreb Cathedral. If you haven't seen in, then you haven't really been to Zagreb. This astonishing building is the tallest structure in the country, and one of Croatia's biggest architectural gems.

Built in the 13th century, the cathedral is well known for its prominent spires, which are visible from almost any part of the city. The building itself was severely damaged several times throughout its long existence, including being devastated in an 1880 earthquake. However, the cathedral was successfully restored and today still retains its appealing Gothic look. You really can't miss this significant landmark, since it is located only a few steps from the Manduševac fountain.

While you are exploring this quaint area, make sure to visit the Church of St. Mark. Gracing a lovely St. Mark's Square, this church is a great example of the Romanesque and Gothic architecture. The exact date of its construction is not known, but it was probably built in the 13th century. Decorated with colorful tiles, the facade of this medieval church beautifully showcases the emblem of Zagreb on the right side, and the coat of arms of Croatia, Slavonia and Dalmatia on the left side. The building itself is located in the center of St. Mark's Square, and is open only at Mass times. This charming square is home to many other important buildings, including the seat of the Government of Croatia, the Old City Hall, and Croatian Parliament.

One of the city's most popular museums is also located in the Upper Town. The Museum of Broken Relationships is definitely one of the most emotional and quirkiest museums you could ever visit. As its name implies, it is devoted to failed romances and the sensibility of human relationships. You can see some of the original objects, and unusual exhibits from all around the world, accompanied with a convincing explanation of the relationship, summary of the dates and notes by their donors. The memories and emotions these objects symbolize are certainly worth your attention, so allow 45 minutes here.

Those who are less nostalgic could also visit the Croatian Museum of Naive Art. Housed in the 18th-century Raffay Palace in the Upper Town, this fine art museum displays an impressive collection of paintings, sculptures, drawings and prints from the 1990's. The main highlights are the works of Ivan Generalić, the first Croatian naive painter. If you pre-book in advance, then a guide is available in English.

Among the several pleasant galleries in this historic area, Klovićevi Dvori Gallery is well worth the detour for its impressive exhibits and collections. Housed in a former Jesuit monastery from the 17th century, this notable gallery is named after the famous Croatian artist Juraj Julije Klović. The gallery features mainly contemporary fine art, while its charming gift shop is a great place to purchase some original souvenirs.

If you are after something really special, then you have to see the Lotrščak Tower. This imposing fortified structure was built in the 13th century to protect the town gates. What is truly unique about it is the legendary Gric cannon, and its long tradition. If you hear an intensely loud sound of cannon fire while in Zagreb, don't be afraid. It just indicates it's midday. One of the lesser known facts is that this sharp sound restrained the Turkish invasion of the city. After that powerful cannon bang, Turkish soldiers ran away without invading the city. Therefore, ever since the 19th century, the cannon has been firing from the Tower Lotrščak to mark midday. It is important to note that these shots aren't dangerous in any way. Today, the tower houses a gallery, while the spectacular 360-degree view from the top is well worth the climb.

Near this magnificent tower is a funicular railway, locally known as Uspinjaca. Built in 1890, this is one of the most celebrated attractions of Zagreb. Although Uspinjaca is the shortest funicular in the world, it still delights its visitors. The lower station is situated on Tomiceva Street, while the upper station is located near the Lotršcak Tower. Obviously the main purpose of this blue funicular is to connect the Lower and Upper Towns, but its cultural importance is invaluable. The funicular runs daily, and you can purchase your ticket at the operator's booth near the lower station.

Before you leave this picturesque area, make sure to visit the Church of St. Catherine. Situated on the Catherine's Square in the Upper Town, this Baroque church is one of the most beautiful structures in the city. Built in the 17th century, the Church of St. Catherine is well known for its opulent stucco reliefs and sumptuous Baroque altars. If you are a Christian, perhaps you would also love to visit the place of exceptional importance. Situated in the Upper Town, the Stone gate (Kamenita vrata), is the only preserved gate that once connected the Lower town to the Upper town. The painting of Virgin Mary you will see here is the only item that miraculously survived the 1731 fire. If you ask me, this narrow passage is the most exceptional place in Zagreb, with the soothing energy, where you can pray, light a candle, and feel fully content.

If you will be spending some extra time in Zagreb, you can now plan to explore the city even further. Located right next to the King Tomislav Square, and near the Central Rail Station, there is an imposing yellow building that leaves everyone in absolute awe. This exceptional massive structure is actually the Art Pavilion, which is now used for temporary exhibitions of contemporary art. This is also an art gallery where you can see some truly fantastic works by the famous Croatian artist Ivan Meštrovic. If you decide to stroll around this area, check out the square of King Tomislav, which is famous for its statue commemorating the first King of Croatia.

Next, you could even explore the Zagreb Botanical Garden, which is located right next to the Esplanade Hotel. A pleasant and beautiful sight, it offers a unique collection of interesting plants as well as various large ponds. Founded in 1889, this peaceful place is very well organized and makes for a very pleasant stroll. It is not the biggest attraction in Zagreb, to be sure, but of some interest if you are in the city.

Around the country there are certain buildings that are architectural gems you should add to your travel bucket list. The Croatian National Theatre in Zagreb, known under the acronym HNK is one of them. Located in the Lower Town, on Marshal Tito Square, this neobaroque building regularly stages opera, music and ballet performances. It was established in 1895, while the building itself was designed by the famous Viennese architects Ferdinand Fellner and Herman Helmer. At the entrance of the building you will notice Ivan Meštrovic's wall sculpture The Source of Life.

As the largest park in the city, Maksimir Park and Zagreb Zoo just begs you to walk around. This is a great place to amble along the small lakes, perhaps stopping for a picnic, or possibly spending some time at the 85-year old Zoo. A family favorite, the Zoo is situated right within the Maksimir Park and features a huge number of animal species, as well as a petting zoo. This peaceful spot is easily accessible by tram. Trams run in both directions approximately every 10 minutes, but generally much more often. From the main railway station, you can reach the zoo on the #4 tram line towards the Dubrava/Dubec station. Get off at the Bukovacka station, walk a bit further along the road, and you will see the Maksimir Park on your left and, the Maksimir Stadium on your right. Built in 1912, this stadium is the home of Dinamo Zagreb, the best football team in the country. Also, it is sometimes used as the venue for some large-scale concerts.

If you still have the stamina after exploring the Maksimir Park, you may want to visit the city's wonderful lakes. Jarun Lake is a large recreational area with 6 islands, and a huge range of recreational opportunities. The clear waters are perfect for rowing, paddle boarding, sailing, surfing, and swimming, so Jarun is extremely popular at any time of the year, but especially in summer. The heart of this charming area is the actual lake itself, which is often used for different activities.

Jarun also boasts miles and miles of footpaths and cycling lanes, and many pebble beaches, alongside which are numerous popular bars and restaurants. Each summer, Lake Jarun also hosts a music festival on its shores – the INmusic Festival. You can reach this popular place with tram lines 17 (which goes through the central square of Ban Jelacic) and 5. Get off at the station called Jarun and then follow the signs until you reach the lake.

Another interesting park to visit is Bundek. It has a charming lake and is host to firework festivals, botanical manifestations, music festivals and concerts. Here you will be able to be entertained by outdoor activities such as fishing and swimming. You can access from the city center by catching any of the buses going in the direction of Novi Zagreb, and get off at the station called Bundek.

One of the city's most prestigious places is the Mirogoj Cemetery. It was opened in 1876 north of the city center, on Mirogojska Road. The Mirogoj Cemetery is a major tourist attraction, renowned for its arcades, pavilions, monuments, and tombs, and it is often hailed as the most famous cemetery in Zagreb. Among the famous people buried there are Franjo

Tudman, Miroslav Krleza, and Branko Gavella. The best option to reach this place is to take a taxi from the city center.

A visit to the mountain called Medvednica is a must when you go to Zagreb. This is a great place for a hike, and offers spectacular views of the city and its surroundings. Medvednica Mountain is one of the most famous nature parks in the country, and there is a large winter sports center on the northern slopes towards Sljeme.

Medvednica is widely known for hosting several important events, including the annual FIS World Cup skiing races, known as the Snow Queen Trophy or Snjezna Kraljica. Many amateurs and skiers of all levels continue to flock here to breathe fresh mountain air. Sljeme is the highest point of the area, at an elevation of 1,033 m above sea level. The area offers everything you could possibly need for your mountain trip, including T-bar lifts. One of the biggest attractions here is the Veternica cave in the southwestern part of Medvednica. This is a wonderful place to explore if you have an extra day in your schedule. However, getting here is half the battle, so I would recommend taking a taxi.

Where to stay in Zagreb

You will have no trouble finding a place to lay your head here in Zagreb, with many great options in every price range. As one of the most popular destinations in Croatia, Zagreb is ready to welcome tourists any time of the year with a wide range of accommodation options - from luxurious hotels to youth hostels and a lot of mid range solutions in between, and catering for everybody's needs, taste and budget.

Despite being one of the most expensive cities in Croatia, it is still possible to find cheap accommodation around the city, especially if you are on a budget or if you simply would rather spend your money in the best restaurants or on the exciting shows that this eclectic city has on offer every day. Zagreb is home to many fabulous luxury hotels, and charming boutique hotels, but the capital is also packed with budget accommodation and friendly hostels.

Most visitors to Zagreb like to stay within the city center, an area which contains the highest concentration of attractions and things to see. This area of Zagreb is well served by public transport though besides beautiful buildings, it is also home to numerous night clubs, shops, restaurants and bars. Many of Zagreb's hotels cater to business travelers, so special deals and discounts are often available.

The Esplanade Zagreb Hotel

If you are looking for a historic luxury hotel in the heart of Croatia's capital, then look no further - the Esplanade Zagreb Hotel has become something of an unofficial city symbol. It is conveniently located near the central railway station of Zagreb, so it is perfect for guests who want elegant comfort along with convenience and a historic location right near the Zagreb Botanical Garden. This charming hotel was constructed in 1925 to provide accommodation for travellers of the well known Orient Express train. Today, this elegant beauty still continues to surprise its guests with its spectacular Oleander Terrace and superb facilities. As one of the best hotels in Croatia, the Esplanade Zagreb Hotel is a favorite spot for celebrities. Many of them have stayed there, including Alfred Hitchcock, Elizabeth Taylor, Louis Armstrong, Woody Allen, and many others.

No wonder this luxury hotel has a lot to offer, including a terrific location, an elegant look, and exceptional service. Expect spacious, beautifully decorated rooms with free Wi-Fi internet access. Along with a restaurant, you will find a health club, a bar, a sauna, and a steam room. If all this doesn't sound relaxing enough, there is a small public seating area with beautiful fountain right next to the hotel.

(Address: Mihanoviceva ul. 1, 10000, Zagreb)

Sheraton Zagreb Hotel

This legendary hotel, in league with the Esplanade, is the best choice for those who love modern, elegant style, and superior service. Sheraton Hotel Zagreb is located in a modern area that's about a 10-minute walk from the center of the city (or a super-quick ride on the blue tram). However, this opulent hotel offers everything you could ask for.

The hotel features 2 pleasant restaurants where you can sample both Croatian and international dishes, a casino, a health club, a bar, and an indoor heated pool. Public spaces are a visually attractive mix of high ceilings, and opulence, while the elegant, spacious rooms are beautifully furnished, and are filled with amenities, and thoughtful touches like pillow menus and bathrobes.

(Address: Ul. kneza Borne 2, 10000, Zagreb)

Westin Zagreb Hotel

Westin Hotel Zagreb is a great place to stay if you are looking for a calm place to relax and rejuvenate. Its facilities, along with the fact that Westin is nicer than most hotels, make it a prime target for business travellers. This elegant 5-star hotel is centrally located in the very center of the city. It is situated near the Mimara Museum, and the National Theatre.

All of the rooms have satellite TV, free WiFi, and minibars. The hotel features a full-service spa with several wellness treatments, a casino, and a restaurant. There is also an indoor pool, a health club, and a bar.

(Address: Ul. Izidora Kršnjavog 1, 10000, Zagreb)

Hotel Dubrovnik

Located on Ban Jelacic Square, right in the heart of the city, Hotel Dubrovnik is one of the best places to stay if this is your first visit to Zagreb. Built in 1929, this 4-star hotel is within easy walking distance of Dolac Market, Zagreb Cathedral, Zagreb Eye Viewpoint, and many other top attractions. The main shopping area, Ilica Street is also right near the hotel.

The hotel offers a restaurant, a fitness center and a bar. There is also a 24-hour business center, and a coffee shop. The style inside is a marriage of modern comfort and traditional charm. The spacious rooms are air-conditioned, and each features a TV with digital channels and a minibar. Free Wi-Fi is also available. Ask for a room off the street if noise affects your sleep, because this area is often very lively.

(Address: Gajeva ul. 1, 10000, Zagreb)

Where to satisfy your cravings

Numerous eateries and restaurants in Zagreb offer various cuisines as they aim to satisfy diverse individual preferences and budgets. The ever-changing culinary scene in Zagreb boasts an eclectic mix of fine-dining restaurants, pizzerias, gastro pubs, cafes and bistros, which offer a wide range of local and international delicacies. Zagreb's eateries set high standards in terms of the quality of food served and great places to eat can be found throughout the city.

Bistro Rouge Marin

Located in a restored factory amid residential blocks near the Radnicka Street, this restaurant is guaranteed to exceed your expectations. Consistently voted one of Zagreb's greatest eateries, for its excellent service and its delicious focus on gourmet burgers and bistro fare, it definitely shouldn't be missed. It is a good place to unwind with a bottle of wine, a good coffee, or a delicious cheeseburger. I favor their muscat pumpkin risotto and ham with mascarpone cream and Japanese sansho pepper, but you might also consider their

Chapter 6: Croatia Proper

Anyone who knows anything about Croatia would certainly have heard something about Croatia Proper. Croatia proper encompasses several smaller areas in the country, including Medimurje, Turopolje, and Zumberak. Also, it is one of the four historical regions of Croatia, and stretches between Slavonia in the east, the Adriatic Sea in the west, and Dalmatia to the south. Zagreb is part of this historical region as well, but there are more beautiful places worth seeing.

Situated in the Zagreb metropolitan area, Samobor is located 24 kilometers west of Zagreb. It is a charming medieval town with beautiful old core and many hidden attractions. Featuring a wide range of cultural treasures, Sabomor is a great place to visit any time of the year. Many Croatian artists flocked to Samobor seeking inspiration for their works of art. Visiting this quaint, medieval town is like taking a step back in time.

Because of its relatively small size, Samobor is also a great place to explore on foot. Its spectacular location makes it a great destination for outdoor lovers as there are so many wonderful activities, including hiking and walking. If you would rather take in the scenic view from a distance, you could visit an abandoned fortification called Samobor's Old Town. It is situated on the scenic Tepec hill. The fort was built in the 13th century by supporters of Czech King Otokar. Although it was abandoned in the 18th century, today it serves as a charming attraction.

The streets of this charming town are packed with interesting shops and gorgeous buildings. In the oldest section of the city you can visit the Church of St. Mihalj. This beautiful Gothic church was first mentioned in the 16th century, and restored and rebuilt in the 17th century. It is devoted to St. Michael, and features a lovely altar from the Baroque period.

A must-visit for any Samobor guest is the Samobor Museum. This immensely interesting museum contains a great collection of exhibits related to Samobor's geological, archeological, ethnographic, and cultural history. There are various walking tours worth taking to explore attractions such as the Samobor Museum, and the Liberation Park, which is dedicated to Croatian soldiers who died in the Homeland War.

Home to many unique buildings and art galleries, this medieval town also hosts many festivals throughout the year, including the Samobor Carnival. The town actually has some of the most interesting and entertaining events in the region. From medieval to strange to quaint, you are bound to find something that piques your attention.

Before you leave Samobor, make sure to try the famous "kremšnite". It is one of Croatia's most famous desserts. If you haven't tried this cake, then you haven't really been in Samobor.

Another charming town in this amazing region is called Karlovac. It was built in the 16th century by the archduke Charles II Francis of Austria as a military bastion against the Turks. Karlovac is as beautiful today as it was back then. The town is famous for its four beautiful rivers and numerous parks and green areas. Therefore, it is the perfect spot to unwind by the water.

If you decide to visit Karlovac, make sure to explore the old part of the city locally known as Zvijezda to absorb the beauty of the old buildings that now house a variety of stores, shops, and mouthwatering restaurants. For those wanting to explore

Chapter 7: Split - the city with a thousand faces

Split is the second largest city in the country and is noted for its many white sand beaches, Diocletian's Palace, and rich history. Nestled on the eastern side of the Adriatic Sea, Split is also the largest city in the region of Dalmatia. It is ideally surrounded by the ridges Kozjak and the neighbouring Mosor, while the legendary Marjan hill proudly rises in the western side of the peninsula.

As one of the oldest cities in the country, Split has a rich history. In 305 AD, the famous Roman Emperor Diocletian, decided to construct a palace in the scenic location which eventually turned into the second largest city in the country - Split. This picturesque city witnessed a huge development that progressed over the years. Today, Split is a bustling city with beautiful landmarks, stunning beaches and vibrant neighborhoods.

Most visitors to Split are holiday makers who book a vacation to Split to swim in the warm Adriatic sea, and to explore its numerous interesting attractions that include several treasure filled museums and galleries, a rich culinary and cultural heritage, a vibrant nightlife scene, great shopping options and easy access to amazing beaches. The city also features a historic, picturesque promenade with charming architectural gems and lots of interesting sights.

Getting around Split

The Split Airport, commonly known as Resnik Airport is the second most important international airport in the country. It is situated approximately 25 km from Split, in the town of Kaštela. From the airport, you can reach Split by bus, taxi or car rentals. The Airport bus is the best value for transport between the airport and the city. Bus number 37 will also take you from the airport to your city lodging. You can buy your tickets directly from the driver. Taxis also wait outside the airport terminal, and the journey between the airport and city center takes around 30 minutes.

Surprisingly, Split is best discovered on foot, and the sights can be explored in less than half a day. A great place to start is at the Riva, Split's seafront promenade, which runs through the old town. From here walk to the harbor if interested.

Where to sleep in Split

Hotels in Split are located all over the city in its numerous colorful neighborhoods. However, most visitors to Split tend to stay in the city's downtown area, which is really compact and easily navigable by foot. This part of the city also has the largest concentration of hotels, which cater to all tastes and preferences. Depending on your individual desires, you can choose to stay in one of these excellent hotels.

Palace Judita Heritage Hotel

It is hard to find the words to properly describe this charming hotel that is committed equally to its guests and rich heritage. Set in a charming old palace from the 16th century, Palace Judita Heritage Hotel is still one of my favorite places to stay in Split. There is just something special and welcoming about this place, and for the price, you get superb amenities. Its large and luxurious rooms are air-conditioned and have nice bathrooms. This 4-star hotel is ideally located on the main square, near the famous Diocletian's Palace, and features a bar, concierge services, a library, and dry cleaning. Wi-Fi is also available in the entire hotel.

(Address: Narodni trg 4, 21000, Split)

Hotel Vestibul Palace

There is lots of old-world charm at Hotel Vestibul Palace. Located in the heart of the city, this 4-star hotel truly deserves all the superlatives. It is enclosed by ancient Roman walls, and offers elegant, beautifully decorated rooms with free Wi-Fi and memory foam beds. Rooms and great bathrooms are literally perfect in every detail. In addition, the hotel also features a restaurant, a bar, and valet parking. If you want reliable service and stylish rooms, Hotel Vestibul Palace is your best bet.

(Address: Ul. Iza Vestibula 4, 21000, Split)

Hotel Luxe Split

If you favor the peace and quiet, then the sublime Hotel Luxe Split is for you. It is one of the most notable hotels in the city and one of my favorites. This 4-star hotel has earned its reputation for great service in a prime location, and if you prefer luxury, you will love the classy environment. Along with a bar, this charming hotel has a fitness center and a spa tub. Free buffet breakfast and free WiFi are also provided. Additionally, the hotel features a sauna, and massage rooms. All rooms are beautifully decorated and equipped with LED satellite TVs.

(Address: Ul. kralja Zvonimira 6, 21000, Split)

Where to satisfy your cravings

As the second largest city in the country, Split has many excellent restaurants in all price ranges scattered through the city. The Riva in particular is a good place to dine.

Paradigma Restaurant

In contrast to most restaurants in the city, Paradigma offers Croatian and Mediterranean cuisine in an upmarket, fashionable interior. Overlooking the Riva promenade, this elegant establishment boasts an impressive wine list, as well as a large selection of beers. Their private rooftop terrace is lovely, with great sea views. Reservations for dinner are recommended.

(Address: Ul. bana Josipa Jelacica 3, 21000, Split)

Bajamonti Restaurant

Situated right in the Prokurative Square, this excellent restaurant is named after the legendary former mayor of Split, who constructed a theater in the 19th century. Today, this popular place serves a wide variety of Mediterranean dishes as well as good coffee and great cakes. The food is great and prices are surprisingly moderate. Try their famous beef risotto with balsamic vinegar, honey, and Mediterranean herbs.

(Address: Marmontova ul. 3, 21000, Split)

Konoba Oštarija u Vidakovi

One of the most authentic restaurants in the city is definitely Konoba Oštarija u Vidakovi. You may prefer to reserve a table at the more upscale restaurants, or visit this intimate establishment for lunch. Situated near the famous Bacvice beach, this typical Croatian restaurant serves some of the best regional dishes in the city. In addition, it has a rustic feel and friendly atmosphere, and generally draws fewer tourists than the restaurants in the old town.

(Address: Prilaz brace Kaliterna 8, 21000, Split)

Where to shop

Shopping is one of the most popular activities in Split. The city's main shopping hubs are located in the Old Town, especially around Diocletian's Palace. In fact, most of this area is packed with shops of all kinds and sizes.

Almost everything you could possibly need can also be found amidst the stalls of the legendary open-air Pazar Market. This charming spot is located at the end of Diocletian's Palace, so it can easily be found.

Another long established shopping spot in Split is Marmontova Street. This bustling street is a shopper's paradise with many chic boutiques and trendy stores, but numerous shops are also found in side streets.

You could also visit Joker, the first shopping mall in Split. It is situated within a 15-minute walk from the city center, on Put Brodarice 6. Here you can find many popular stores like Benetton, Nike, Mustang, and Tom Tailor. There is also a great restaurant, lots of bars and McDonald's. The mall has a large cinema, and an open parking garage which is free of charge.

Attractions that make Split so special

Split offers lots of vibrant atmosphere and enough attractions to convince you to explore it for a couple of days before heading out to the splendid seaside resorts and islands. Most visitors to Split want nothing more than to relax on the beach. The more adventurous visitors enjoy taking advantage of the many activities that this beautiful city has to offer such as parasailing, surfing, boating, swimming and scuba diving.

Split is blessed with a wide array of sight-seeing opportunities as well, and these are ideal for those people who want to take a break from beach side activities and explore the area to learn more about its history, tradition and culture.

Your visit to Split will probably revolve around the iconic Diocletian's Palace. This is where you will find numerous passageways, courtyards, and some of the finest boutiques and dining establishments in the city. Yes, there are some landmarks that stand head and shoulders above the rest, and Diocletian's Palace is one of them. It is the beating heart and soul of Split, a meeting place for residents and tourists from around the world.

This splendid and massive structure was built by the Roman emperor Diocletian to project his absolute wealth. It was constructed between the late 3rd and the early 4th centuries A.D. The palace has undergone relatively few modifications since its construction, though the original building was revamped in the Middle Ages. This huge complex actually looks like a large fortified town, and is one of the best preserved Roman palaces in the world.

Two central streets, cardo and decumanus, lead to the central area of the complex, known as the Peristyle. Nearby, you can see the Temple of the Aesculapius, and the Temple of Jupiter which was converted into a baptistery. One of the most popular attractions though is a black sphinx, which was brought here all the way from Egypt. There are numerous buildings, statues, and interesting sights within the complex boundaries, so you should definitely take enough time to explore it to make the most of your visit.

The Cathedral of Saint Domnius, or St. Duje's cathedral is also one of the most celebrated attractions in Split. It was originally constructed in the 4th century as a mausoleum for Diocletian, and is regarded as the oldest cathedral in the world still in use. This imposing cathedral is famous for its stunning bell tower which gives you a magnificent view of the city and its surroundings.

The best place to enjoy the beauty of nature in Split is the legendary Marjan hill. It is a great place for long walks, hikes, and bike rides where one can relax for hours and forget about everything else. Marjan's highest point, Telegrin is the perfect spot to escape the hectic city life and enjoy a relaxing atmosphere. From the top, you have a great view over the city and its surroundings. In case you want to spend your precious time lying on the beach, some of the finest beaches in the city, including Kasjuni beach are located at the foot of Marjan hill.

Split has many excellent museums, including the Ethnographical Museum which displays a plethora of ethnographic items, and the Croatian Maritime Museum which boasts a large collection of maritime and nautical equipment. One of the best museums in Split though, is the Archaeological Museum. It is the oldest museum in the country dating back to 1820. The museum displays many artifacts and exhibits from the Roman period.

The symbolic center of Split, though is its long seafront promenade, locally known as the Riva. This charming area is decorated with white marble pathways and palms, and includes a variety of restaurants, bars, and shops. With a wide range of different adventures, opportunities and things to do in Split, taking a stroll along the promenade is one of the best experiences you can have.

Chapter 8: Magnificent places to visit in Dalmatia

Thanks mostly to its dramatic location, beautiful beaches, and stunning islands that are especially enchanting during summertime, Dalmatia is well-known as one of Croatia's most alluring regions. It stretches all the way to the Bay of Kotor, in the south. Some of the most beautiful islands are located in this region, such as Hvar and Korcula, so this inviting region is a haven for water sports enthusiasts, celebrities, and most of all holidaymakers. Whether you are looking for active destinations or more seclusion, Dalmatia certainly has something for you.

The biggest cities in Dalmatia are Split, Zadar, Dubrovnik and Šibenik. Many of these well-known cities get crowded or too touristy, but they are still absolutely breathtaking. If you get tired of the sand and sea, Dalmatia also has plenty more to offer. The region is well-known for its delightful national parks, so you could visit one of them as well. From the Makarska Riviera to the farthest reaches of the Dubrovnik–Neretva County, there are plenty of seaside towns and resorts to please visitors in search of pristine beaches, dramatic shorelines, Roman ruins, art, nightlife, culture, and delicious cuisine.

One of the largest rivers in the country, Neretva, is an ideal place to recharge the batteries before heading to the coast. Neretva is famous for its rich flora and fauna, as well as cultural and historic heritage. To get the most out of your visit to Dalmatia, I would recommend renting a car in Split, Zadar, or Šibenik. You will have absolute freedom to visit and explore all those hidden wonders in this absolutely breathtaking region.

Hvar

Hvar is the country's most luxurious and expensive island, and for good reason. This romantic Adriatic jewel is the epitome of wealth, glitz, and glamour. Hvar regularly attracts the world's most powerful jet set. Wondering why? The answer is pretty simple. Visiting Hvar can feel like visiting Monte Carlo, and, best of all, you can easily reach it with either ferry or catamaran from Split. Undoubtedly, Hvar is one of the best places to visit in Croatia, as long as you can afford it.

Despite Hvars' hedonistic flair, there is enough natural attractions to make a trip worthwhile. Nestled between the islands of Brac, Vis, and Korcula, Hvar is well known for its lavender fields, green pine forests, numerous vineyards, olive groves, and fruit orchards. Every part of this island is even more beautiful than the other. This means that you will have plenty of opportunities to explore the surrounding nature, and enjoy the atmosphere this beautiful island has to offer.

Thanks to its marvelous location and extreme natural beauty, Hvar has been inhabited ever since the earliest prehistoric times. Therefore, you will have plenty of opportunities to combine some great sightseeing with your beach vacation. Some of the best places you should definitely visit are Jelsa, Starigrad, and Hvar town itself.

Hvar town in particular is the main tourist hotspot. During the summer months, its charming port is packed with glamorous yachts. In addition, Hvar with its numerous beaches is a water sports enthusiast's paradise since it offers a huge range of water sports that include wind surfing, sailing, kayaking, surfing, scuba diving, snorkeling and swimming. The town is enclosed by defensive walls, and has a large number of beautiful Venetian palaces and buildings. However, more modern architecture has seen immense urban sprawl over the past two decades.

Hvar's main sightseeing attraction is the Fortress Fortica Španjola. It was built in the late 15th century, in order to protect the city against Turks. Today, this massive fortification houses a collection of amphora and other valuable items from antiquity and the Middle Ages. It also provides an impressive panoramic view of the town of Hvar. You can reach this fort if you walk from the old town, just follow the signs from the main square.

If this ancient structure didn't impress you, you might want to visit the second fortress, known as the Fort Napoleon. It is situated right above the town of Hvar, but you should need to take a taxi to get to the fortress. Hvar also has one of the oldest theatres in Europe. It was constructed in 1612, and is located in the center of the historical area of Hvar.

The Cathedral of Sv. Stjepan from the 14th century is also worth your attention. This remarkable structure beautifully showcases the Dalmatian architecture. It is situated on the eastern side of the main square, at the end of the Pjaca. From here, you could also visit the Paladini Palace, and the Clock Tower.

One of the best places you could visit is the Franciscan Monastery from the 15th century. It was built as a calm shelter for sailors. The monastery is well known for its extravagant bell tower, and the cloister, with its huge monumental rounded arches. The adjoining church, named Our Lady of Mercy, houses some fine paintings and exhibits, so you should definitely check it out.

Depending on your taste, you will find that Hvar is not the cheapest place to stay. However, Hvar features a wide array of accommodation options that range from luxury hotels to boutique, discount hotels, private accommodation units, and budget accommodation.

Hvar also offers a wide range of restaurants, though many visitors think that the prices charged by most restaurants here are quite high compared to similar restaurants in other parts of Croatia. Nevertheless, there are plenty of great restaurants, especially around the promenade to choose from. If you fancy fine dining, explore the streets around the main square. The night scene here is very unique, as it caters to those with deep pockets. If you want to dance the night away, there is no better place to be than Veneranda Club. This open-air club is one of the best party venues in Europe.

A visit to one of the beaches around the island is a great way to cool off during the island's long and hot summer. Hvar is actually the sunniest island in Croatia. If you are looking for some truly breathtaking beaches, then I would recommend visiting the Pakleni islands where you will find various beautiful beaches, including a sandy beach. If you need a short weekend escape, Hvar has a lot of smaller beaches on each side of the town.

Zadar

Zadar is a place where you can feel at home. Even if this is your first visit you will feel like you know this city. It is true that Zadar shares its everlasting appeal with other towns in this region, but it also has some pretty special characteristics of its own. Zadar's flair and its unique vibe attract millions of visitors every year. At the same time, however, Zadar is a family-friendly city characterised by its rich history, its excellent transport links, its attractive streets with lots of green spaces and sweeping Adriatic Sea beaches, and the most appealing sunset in the world.

It is really not surprising that Alfred Hitchcock left his heart here. He once said that Zadar has the most astonishing sunset in the world. Travellers from all over the globe know why Zadar is so magical, so it shouldn't come as much of a surprise that Zadar is one of the most unique cities in Croatia.

There is a lot to see and experience on your visit to Zadar. With numerous sights and landmarks within close proximity you will certainly fill your visit with plenty of activities that Zadar has to offer. One of the best places to get a real sense of Zadar's rich heritage is the Church of Saint Donatus. The church was built in the 9th century, and is well known for its unique, pre-Romanesque shape. Its design is mainly characterised by simplicity resulting in a unique architecture typical for this region. Today, the church has been used for concerts, events, and rehearsals including the annual International Festival of Medieval Renaissance Music.

Also of note is the forum which is situated right in front of the Church of Saint Donatus. It was constructed by the Roman Emperor Augustus between the second half of the first century and the third century. Although this complex is ruined, some columns are still standing.

Nearby, you could also visit the Cathedral of St. Anastasia. It was constructed in the 12th and 13th centuries. One of the most striking features of this imposing cathedral is its lavishly decorated facade designed in the Romanesque style. This is the largest cathedral in the region, and certainly one of the most beautiful structures in the country. The building was heavily destroyed during the Second World War, and has since been restored.

Cool, unique and iconic are just a few of the words that can be used to describe the sights and landmarks in Zadar. The Sea Organ or Morske Orgulje, designed by the famous architect Nikola Bašic, converts the movement of the water into a special, soothing melody. The gentle waves are pushing air through more than 30 pipes of diverse lengths, creating relaxing and atmospheric sounds. If you only have a day or two, make sure you check out this remarkable symbol of Zadar.

This spectacular city was once the biggest fortified city in the Republic of Venice, so make sure to visit its old walls and historic portals near the splendid Foša harbor. The Land Gate, one of the best preserved portals, is considered as the most visually appealing.

This part of Dalmatia has several romantic towns which make interesting day trips within easy reach of Zadar. Biograd, Benkovac, and Nin all have lots of architecture and numerous attractions worth seeing as well as attractive old towns where you can have a drink and enjoy a very traditional atmosphere. Steeped in history, culture, and uniqueness, Zadar is certainly the best destination for all to embrace Croatia at its very best.

Šibenik

Šibenik is a beautiful and well-preserved historic city in Dalmatia. When compared to Zadar, Šibenik doesn't initially stand out as a cradle of culture. But if you look closer, you will find that Šibenik is just as astonishing as Zadar. Šibenik is the oldest city in this part of Croatia, and the main tourist hub of Šibenik–Knin County. The city boasts jaw-dropping beaches, world-class cuisine, cozy restaurants and plenty of booming nightlife venues. Šibenik is also a great base for numerous day trips, including visits to the Krka National Park, and the Kornati archipelago.

And then there is the city's historic appeal. History buffs should tour the forts of St. Michael, St. John and Šubićevac, as well as the Cathedral of St. James. This imposing cathedral is the most significant architectural structure of the Renaissance in Croatia. It took more than 100 years to complete the cathedral's construction. This only shows how important this structure really is. The medieval exterior of the Cathedral of St. James has a solid and sturdy look. During the War of Independence, the dome of the cathedral was seriously destroyed, but it was subsequently reconstructed. Inside, the main highlight is the Altar of the Holy Three Kings. Today, this awe-inspiring basilica has been inscribed on UNESCO's World Heritage List.

The Cathedral of St. James is a must-see, but a visit to St. Nicholas Fortress should also be high on your list. This majestic fortress is one of the most important examples of defense architecture in the region. It was originally built in the 16th century to prevent an expected Turkish attack. Today, St. Nicholas Fortress is one of the best places in Šibenik to watch the sunset.

Families can enjoy a day at the Medieval Garden of St Lawrence Monastery. It is the only garden of its kind in the country, and is well known for its dramatic vistas. This magical garden is home to a wealth of exciting, and useful medical plants and herbs. There is even a lovely cafe with outdoor seating where you can relax and unwind.

Instead of spending all your time around the city centre, you can discover a more traditional side of Šibenik by simply strolling through the vibrant Zaton settlement. Šibenik may be small, but it is packed with a plethora of activities that will surely please history buffs, foodies and curious travelers of all ages. Ultimately, the city's beautiful green areas and proximity to excellent natural attractions and small villages make it one of the most desirable cities for adventure travelers.

Vodice

Vodice is Croatia's well known party destination, a long-established tourist resort that has been attracting holidaymakers since the 19th century. Once a thriving Venetian town known as Arausa, Vodice transformed into one of the most popular summer destinations in the country. Situated in the Šibenik-Knin County, this picturesque town is renowned for its liveliness and great tourist facilities. With endless bars, restaurants, beaches, and frequent boat services, Vodice caters for anyone seeking a lively getaway.

There are wonderful outdoor activities for fun loving families, and numerous nightclubs for party lovers who want to dance the night away. You can also find a wide array of accommodation options in Vodice, from luxury hotels to self-catering apartments.

Note that there aren't many specific attractions in the town, although there are plenty of panoramic vistas and delightful spots. Vodice has a small but charming historic centre, and is within easy reach of a plethora of more peaceful Croatian towns and islands. If you are travelling from Šibenik, there are frequent buses and ferries running to Vodice.

The town is known for its crystal clear waters and pebble and sandy beaches, but there are also plenty of attractions nearby. The old town of Vodice is well worth exploring as well. It has several remains of defensive walls that protected the town from the Turks, as well as some beautiful churches from the 18th century. The heart of Vodice is the harbor, which is jam packed with restaurants, boutiques, souvenir shops, and charming cafes where you can sit and watch the world go by.

Many tourists visit Vodice in its own right, many more use the town as a base for exploring the region. The town's position makes it ideal for boat trips. A trip out to the offshore islets of Logorun and Tijat is a great way to take a break from the hustle and bustle of Vodice. This coastal gem is also a great base for taking an excursion to the National Park Krka, Kornati National Park, Vransko Lake Nature Park, Šibenik, or the splendid islands of Prvić and Zlarin.

Dubrovnik

Dubrovnik is the most popular tourist destination in the country, and it is easy to see why. A Unesco World Heritage

Site since 1979, the city is located at the southern end of Croatia. No matter your preferences, it is safe to say Dubrovnik won't leave you unsatisfied.

While in Dubrovnik, you can indulge in the archaeological delights of the impressively preserved stone walls or discover a mish-mash of culture flourishing throughout Dubrovnik's bustling streets. Without any false modesty, this pearl of the Adriatic is one of the greatest vacation destinations in the world. However, Dubrovnik as we know it today wasn't always so peaceful. During the Homeland War, the city was brutally besieged by the Yugoslav People's Army. If you are interested in learning more about the city's history, there are two museums devoted to this painful period of Croatia's past. The Memorial Room of Dubrovnik Defenders displays pictures of young soldiers who gave their life for our freedom, while the Museum of Croatian War of Independence offers a glimpse of the city's heartbreaking past. The museum houses numerous exhibits, including documents, art and documentary photographs from the 1990's.

Looking at the splendid museums, fancy restaurants, and the blossoming nightlife scene, you might find it hard to believe that just two decades ago, this bustling Croatian city was almost completely devastated.

You will also want to visit the city's other sights, particularly the old defense grid and, of course, the Sponza Palace. Over the years, the Walls of Dubrovnik were modified, but they are still amongst the best defense systems of the Middle Ages because they were never breached. The walls were built in the 14th and 15th centuries, but were continually expanded and they even withstand a huge earthquake in 1667. The Minčeta Tower is the highest point of the walls, and offers a spectacular panoramic view of the city.

On the other hand, the St. John Fortress houses an aquarium, as well as the Maritime Museum, while the walls of the old St. Lawrence Fortress are almost 12 metres thick. This massive structure was one of the strongest enemies to all aggressors. Also worth mentioning is the fact that these walls were famous even before the hit TV series 'Game of Thrones'.

From glamorous to historic, this awe-inspiring city offers visitors a wide range of interesting attractions. One of the most impressive buildings in the city is the splendid Sponza Palace. It was built in the 16th century, and was unaffected by a major earthquake occurring in the 17th century.

Dubrovnik boasts a lot of historical importance, but the city has some other attractions as well. Its picture-perfect beaches and emerald green waters are perfect for swimming and sunbathing, while numerous boat tours are also available. The Banje beach in particular qualifies as one of the most relaxing and enchanting beaches in the city. Dubrovnik is also well known for its excellent canoeing, scuba diving and boating opportunities.

When it comes to fine dining in Dubrovnik, there are many delectable restaurants that will surprise every guest. However, some of the beachfront restaurants are extremely expensive. For a more traditional and budget-friendly meal, try one of the old-town tavernas. In the end, no book could properly describe the beauty of this ancient city. Neither can it describe the emotion that Dubrovnik leaves in one who has strolled along its narrow streets.

Makarska

Physically, Makarska is situated on a horseshoe shaped bay and features some fine beaches, whitewashed houses, and a hilly terrain dotted with olive trees. Nestled between the Biokovo Mountains and the Adriatic Sea, this charming town is encircled by two peninsulas, called St. Peter and Osejava. As one of the most unspoiled coastal towns in Croatia, Makarska is perfect for those who want a relaxing vacation without any hassle.

Many people have been drawn to this idyllic part of Croatia since the 1900's and it is easy to conclude why. Makarska is the base of the Makarska Riviera, and offers an upbeat mix of palm trees, blue waters, rich greenery, and huge tourist capacities.

The outcome is a charming place brimming with entrancing spots and hidden corners where you could cheerfully spend days or even weeks. Makarska doesn't really have any unmissable tourist attractions; instead the town itself is the biggest attraction. Almost everything in Makarska revolves around its long, charming promenade where cozy cafes, restaurants and shops overlook the splendid harbor.

Makarska is also one of the warmest places in Croatia, and it can be sweltering in July and August. Luckily, the town regularly wows tourists with its lush scenery, romantic harbor, as well as its bountiful beaches. The main beach in Makarska is nearly two kilometers long, and offers various opportunities for more adventurous visitors including scuba diving, paragliding, and windsurfing. Of course, swimming is a popular activity, but that is not all Makarska has to offer. If you need a break from the beach, you could visit St. Mark's Cathedral or explore the Malacological Museum, which is situated in a 16th-century Franciscan monastery. The museum boasts a large collection of shells from all over the globe.

Makarska may be the most prominent town in this coastal region but its laid-back atmosphere makes it an excellent alternative for those who would like to see a more authentic Croatian town. Taking a trip to the Biokovo Nature Park is a great way to finish your visit to Makarska. Biokovo is a large mountain range, located between the rivers of Cetina and Neretva. Its highest point is St. Jure, which offers an unforgettable view of Makarska and the surrounding islands. This unspoiled area boasts superb trails for hiking, walking and biking, as well as a lovely botanical garden.

Today, many centuries after its founding, Makarska is still one of the most impressive coastal cities of Croatia, noted for its stone-paved streets and many palm trees decorating its long promenade. Because of its supreme natural appeal and huge tourist capacities, the entire region around the city is called the Makarska Riviera.

Chapter 9: Rijeka - An unforgettable city

Situated on the Kvarner Gulf, Rijeka is the third largest city in the country, and an important center for maritime transport and shipbuilding in Europe. As a result, Rijeka is an important destination for the business travellers, and is well known for its shipyards and its exquisite port.

However, Rijeka is far from being a dull, monotonous, tedious destination and the city is a favored vacation destination that is famous for its scenic surroundings, numerous attractions, and cultural events as well as great dining and shopping options. Also, Rijeka is a compact city and the majority of its nightlife options are centered around the famous Korzo promenade. Rijeka's charm tends to overshadow its many neighboring cities, which are spectacular destinations in themselves and well worth a trip.

Rijeka and its surrounding region, has been one of my favorite destinations in Croatia for a long time, so I am very pleased that it is now receiving growing international attention. Rijeka is a city of rich musical scene, interesting sights and unique historical background. If you are visiting Rijeka for the very first time, it is safe to say that your trip will be fantastic.

Getting around Rijeka

Rijeka is a major transportation hub for the entire region, and is well served by its perennially busy Rijeka International Airport, which welcomes flights from all over the world. However, this airport is situated on the nearby island of Krk. Luckily, there is an airport bus which runs from the city center to the airport.

If you are flying to Zagreb, there is a regular bus shuttle service from the Zagreb Pleso Airport to Rijeka. The busy bus terminal in Rijeka is located near the famous Capuchin church, on Zabica Square.

Also, from the central train station in Zagreb there are several daily trains to Rijeka. Train is a popular mode of transport in the country, although the train network isn't that extensive. The railway station in Rijeka is located in 5 Krešimirova Street, at the northern part of the city. Rijeka's tourist information office can be found within the building.

The city, aside from its modern airport, is served by many prominent highways like the A6 motorway, which connects Rijeka to Zagreb via the A1, and the A7 motorway, which links the city with Ljubljana in Slovenia. Most visitors to Rijeka choose not to rent a car as it may be perceived to be more trouble than a convenience due to heavy traffic congestion within the city and expensive parking. However, if you do want to rent a car for your stay in Rijeka, I would recommend making your car rental bookings with a car rental agency before you get to Rijeka so you can get a discount.

As for transport within the city, most of Rijeka's essential attractions are located within easy reach of the city center and are easily navigable on foot, although the city is also equipped with a well developed public transport system which consists of commuter trains, ferry service, taxis, and an extensive bus network.

In my personal opinion, Rijeka has the best taxi service in the country. Taxis are probably the most popular mode of transport in the city because they are cheap, efficient, and reliable. Taxis can be hailed in the street or at designated terminals near the bus station, and at the railway station.

Where to stay in Rijeka

This eclectic city has a wide range of hotels that include historic hotels, family –friendly hotels, bed and breakfast inns and other budget accommodation options.

The Best Western Hotel Jadran

Ideally located by the sea, this 4-star hotel is one of the best hotels in the city. It is a modern hotel with comfortable rooms and tasteful furniture. Their excellent restaurant with the breathtaking view of the sea serves international and Mediterranean cuisine, while the hotel even has a private beach. Free Wi-Fi and free self parking are also available. In addition, several coffee shops, a 24-hour business center, a bar, and a conference center are onsite. The hotel is very popular with international visitors, so I would recommend to book well ahead.

(Address: Šetalište XIII divizije 46, 51000, Rijeka)

Grand Hotel Bonavia

This 125 year old hotel is conveniently located in the heart of the city. Numerous attractions, restaurants, shops and art galleries are only a short walk away. The location of this hotel is really excellent and the glass exterior seduces as much from the outside as from the inside. This completely refurbished 4-star hotel also has stylish air-conditioned rooms with free Wi-Fi. Along with 3 restaurants, the hotel features a fitness center and a bar. In addition, a coffee shop, a sauna, and a 24-hour business center are available. Guests can even take advantage of the fitness centre with saunas for free. Grand Hotel Bonavia is a great choice for travellers interested in sightseeing, and shopping.

(Address: Dolac 4, 51000, Rijeka)

Hotel Continental

Built in 1888, this 3-star hotel is probably the oldest hotel in the city. It is located in the heart of Rijeka, and offers a superb location at a relatively low price. The hotel has a lovely restaurant, a bar with an outdoor terrace, and a coffee shop. Other facilities include meeting rooms, dry cleaning, and laundry services. Free WiFi is also provided. Rooms are spacious and modern, and decorated in an uncluttered way. This is a very pleasant hotel with friendly staff, and one of Rijeka's top addresses.

(Address: Šetalište Andrije Kacica Miošica 1, 51000, Rijeka)

Where to eat

Rijeka offers an extremely vibrant culinary scene, and a wide array of restaurants which cater to all travel budgets. If it's traditional, truly local Istrian food that you are looking for, then you should head to the many restaurants located around the Korzo. This area is much favored by tourists, and features a plethora of restaurants where you can find great food at reasonable prices.

Konoba Municipium

Set in a historic palace, Konoba Municipium is arguably the best restaurant in Rijeka, with a wine list to match. This elegant restaurant serves mainly traditional Croatian cuisine and classical dishes. Portions are decent, the food tasty, prices moderate, and the service is exceptional. If your tastes are more refined, Konoba Municipium is your safest bet.

(Address: Trg Rijecke rezolucije 5, 51000, Rijeka)

Konoba Nebuloza

This charming restaurant is no longer a well-kept secret. It is located in the heart of the city, and serves Croatian cuisine with plenty of seafood specialties. Konoba Nebuloza is justifiably popular, because the food here is on a higher scale than in the majority of traditional restaurants found in Zagreb. Prices here are fairly moderate, while the food is absolutely delicious. Try their famous risotto with Swiss chard.

(Address: Titov trg 2, 51000, Rijeka)

Restaurant Kamov

Housed in the Bonavia Hotel, this fine restaurant is an elegant place with stylish furniture and decoration. All the better hotels in Rijeka have restaurants serving Croatian food, but this one is my favorite. The atmosphere here is surprisingly relaxed, while the food is really top-notch. Dishes tend to be appetizing, prices surprisingly low, while the menu offers mainly Croatian and international specialties.

(Address: Dolac 4, 51000, Rijeka)

Where to shop

Rijeka is a shopper's paradise. The city offers countless shopping opportunities, and has numerous trendy stores, chic boutiques and souvenir shops. Generally, the highest concentration of shops can be found around Korzo, where many new department chains and other major outlets are located. Other areas of the city worth exploring include Zabica and Trsat. Trsat in particular is a popular spot for souvenir shopping.

Apart from the magnificent buildings in Plumbum area, the major attraction is the 4-storey Tower Center. As one of the most popular shopping malls in the country, Tower Center offers over 150 stores and services for the entire family. Among everything else, there is a good multi-screen cinema, gambling arcade, and a huge supermarket. You can reach this popular place on the #2 bus line. Get off at the stop called Janka Polica Kamova.

Korzo is the commercial and cultural heart of the city. This area in the city center is home to various major cultural venues, and is peppered with many great shops and restaurants. Much of the area around this promenade is full of beautiful buildings and attractions. One of them is the Croatian National Theatre Ivan pl. Zajc in Rijeka. This elegant building dates from 1885, although the first theater building in Rijeka was built in the 18th century. If you are an architecture lover, you would love to see it in person.

While you are exploring this area, you could also visit the city's main market or *tržnica*. Don't miss this place if you love to get the feel for real local atmosphere. The market is a great place for specialty delicatessen, and the lively fish market is particularly appealing. The pleasant streets around the market are lined with fast food takeaways and charming tavernas for a quick and traditional lunch.

Nearby, the Modello Palace is another piece of fascinating architecture in Rijeka. This lavish building, together with its beautifully decorated facades were built by the Austrian architects Fellner and Helmer at the same time as the National Theatre in Rijeka. The Modello building is equally beautiful inside, and serves as the gathering place of Rijeka's Italian community.

Also worth mentioning is the St. Vitus Cathedral, which is devoted to the patron Saint and protector of the city. Founded in the 17th century, this charming structure is renowned for its beautiful Baroque and Gothic elements.

The Trsat Castle is also one of the most interesting attractions in Rijeka that should be included in your sightseeing itinerary. Strategically situated on a hill 138 meters above sea level, this imposing structure was completely reconstructed and refurbished in the 19th century.

Also, this bastion offers a magnificent view of the coast and the city below. The Trsat Castle is one of the oldest bastions in Croatia which preserves the characteristics of the early medieval town construction. There is even a small restaurant where you can unwind.

If you are on vacation in Rijeka then the Shrine of Our Lady of Trsat should be a must-see attraction on your list. According to legend, this unique place was founded in 1291 when a small Nazareth Barn appeared here, brought by angels. The house mysteriously disappeared later, but it was then found in Loreto, where it still stands today. Situated at the top of Trsat Hill, this is the biggest pilgrimage centre in the region, frequented by numerous pilgrims from all around the world. While there, be sure to visit the Trsat Park, known for its various indigenous plants.

Before you leave Rijeka, you might want to visit the Torpedo Factory. Did you know that the torpedo was actually invented in this industrial city? First prototypes of a torpedo were made and tested at the Torpedo factory in Rijeka, and then distributed to the world. The remains of this legendary complex still exist, including a well-preserved launch ramp used for testing self-propelled torpedoes.

Chapter 10: The best of Istria & Kvarner

Istria is the westernmost region of Croatia, which comprises the largest part of the Istrian peninsula. It really wouldn't be an exaggeration to say that Istria is one of the most spectacular places in the world. Situated between the Gulf of Trieste and the Kvarner Gulf, this stunning region is famous for its idyllic beaches, charming towns, picturesque fishing villages, luxurious harbors, and crystal-clear waters. If you are looking for a destination with great tourist facilities, but also with a number of islands, Istria is your best bet. However, Istria mainly caters to its affluent visitors, so if you are traveling on a budget, you may want to stay in the neighbouring Kvarner area.

Opatija

Opatija is one of those cities where you come expecting nothing in particular and leave wanting you could take it with you. This elegant city beautifully combines everything you could possibly want – world-class restaurants, stunning landscapes, inviting beaches, and cheerful vibe. In fact, Opatija is full of charm and friendly people. The best way to get to know this opulent city is to walk up and down its narrow streets. Believe me, it is worth it. Located in the Kvarner Bay, approximately 15 km west of Rijeka, this awe-inspiring city was the trendiest seaside resort for the Viennese jet set during the period of the Austro-Hungarian Empire. Today, Opatija boasts a truly inviting atmosphere, with inspiring features including narrow streets, elegant and sumptuous buildings, and many great spots for relaxing walks.

Nestled at the foot of the Mount Ucka, Opatija is the main hub of the Riviera. It is encircled by various hills, charming towns and villages, from Vološko to Lovran. The sheer number of beaches in this area is pretty mind-blowing. And whoever tells you that Opatija doesn't have some beautiful beaches, is lying. Situated in the heart of the city, Slatina beach is one of the most alluring beaches in the entire region. This inviting beach attracts a large number of visitors during the entire year, and has everything you could hope for while relaxing and enjoying in the sun.

If you want to see some of Opatija's most important sights, you should visit the old Abbey of Saint Jacob, locally known as Opatija Sv. Jakova. This beautiful structure was built in the 14th century, and is conveniently located in Saint James's Park. Opatija's name is almost self-explanatory; it is named after this Benedictine abbey.

Next on your list should be the Villa Angiolina, built in the 19th century by Iginio Scarpa. This elegant building marked the start of tourism in Opatija. Throughout its long history, the Villa has welcomed numerous important guests from all over the world, including the Austrian empress Maria Anna, and the Croatian Ban Josip Jelacic. Today, this opulent structure houses the Museum of Croatian Tourism.

If you love food, then you will also love Opatija. And thanks to its plethora of excellent restaurants, you will have no trouble finding delectable international cuisine. Here is almost impossible to find a restaurant that doesn't offer jaw dropping sea views. Great food aside, Opatija's soothing aura is contagious, and has been known to attract tourists seeking inspiration, relaxation or rejuvenation.

Pula

Pula is a place that many travellers to Istria will pass through, whether they arrive by train, or bus, but it is definitely worth visiting. Located at the southern end of the Istria peninsula, Pula is the largest city in the region. Its natural appeal, numerous architectural wonders and crystal clear waters have made Pula an internationally celebrated destination. Still, Pula is often overshadowed by Rijeka and Umag.

This strikingly appealing city is renowned for its stunning landscape, verdant coastline, and numerous Roman ruins and temples. Pula was an important naval base under the Austro-Hungarian Empire, as well as Istria's administrative centre under the Romans, so it has a wide array of well-preserved ancient Roman constructions. The town centre is literally scattered with Roman ruins, the most notable of which is the Pula Arena. This imposing amphitheater was built between 27 BC – 68 AD, and is one of the biggest Roman arenas in the entire world, as well as the only structure of its kind with four side towers.

For most tourists, a glimpse of the exterior of the Arena is sufficient, but you could also visit the 1st-century AD triumphal arch of the Sergii, and the legendary temple of Rome and Augustus. The arch was built as a symbol of the victory at Actium, and is dedicated to the Sergii family.

While in Pula, don't forget to explore the city's old quarter. This charming area is packed with narrow streets, and Renaissance structures. One of the most appealing architectural jewels is the Church of St. Francis. It was built in the 13th century, and is noted for its double pulpit, and beautiful motifs.

If you have enough time, you could also visit the following attractions to round out your visit. The Gate of Porta Gemina, with its beautiful arches once served as the entrance to the city. Today, the gate leads to the Archeological Museum, and is one of the few remaining gates after the city walls were pulled down in the 19th century.

Kids will particularly enjoy the Pula aquarium, the only center for the rehabilitation of sea turtles in the country. Housed in the Austro-Hungarian fortress Verudela, this interesting aquarium features several interesting exhibits, including the Mediterranean exhibition which is particularly exciting.

The city's uniqueness isn't tied only to its rich history and marine life. Pula also features an astonishing mild weather, and numerous beautiful beaches that offer ample opportunities for water-based activities like swimming, wreck diving, snorkeling, sailing, cliff diving, and yachting.

Umag

Umag is a charming coastal town located in Istria. This scenic place along the Adriatic Coast is known for its beauty and diversity. In addition to its striking charm and splendid beaches, the medieval city of Umag hosts some exciting and heavily tourist-trafficked annual events such as the ATP Croatia Open, which is held each July at the stadium of the Stella Maris resort.

Although it was first mentioned in the 7th century, Umag already existed during the rule of the Roman Empire. The town may have lost some of the glamour that it had in the early 20th century when it was a favored destination for many foreigners, but Umag continues to attract its fair share of visitors who come here to enjoy its quaint streets, reliable weather and phenomenal annual events.

Most tourists use Umag as a base for visiting Pula and Rovinj, but it's worth spending a day or two here, strolling around this glitzy town and visiting its more popular attractions. The city's old quarter is the best place to begin your sightseeing tour. Stroll along the narrow cobbled streets and explore the old town walls, which date back to the 10th century. You could also visit the Umag Museum, where you can learn more about the history of Umag and check out numerous exhibitions of ancient pottery and crafts. This interesting museum can be found within the Bishop's Tower, in the south-western section of the old town.

The Church of St. Roch is located at the entrance of the old town, and is one of the most famous attractions of Umag. It was built in the beginning of the 16th century, and is noted for its beautiful oil-painted ceiling. This ancient heart of the city features picturesque, narrow alleys that host closely packed medieval buildings. These ancient structures are often used as stages for concerts and other events.

Umag is full of restaurants and cafes, from rather boring but scenic spots facing the sea to charming little konobas hidden in the town centre. This vibrant town also has many excellent bars and an energetic nightlife, so even if you visit Umag in winter you will still find plenty to keep you entertained for a couple of days.

Porec

Located in the scenic Croatian region of Istria, Porec makes a great base for further exploration of this area along the Istrian Riviera, and remains a favorite weekend getaway spot.

This beautiful town is well known for its long coastline stretching from the Mirna River all the way to Vrsar in the south. For several decades, the coast of Porec has been the most frequently visited tourist destination in the country. With its fine restaurants, trendy shops, cozy hotels, and late night club scene, this ancient Roman town is one of the most popular summer resorts in Croatia. It is also one of the most historically enticing towns, whose charms are undeniable. The town has been a seaside destination since the early 1970's.

Regardless of whether you are a first time visitor or frequently keep coming back to Porec, you will certainly have a memorable time. Popular with families, and young partygoers, Porec is also a good place to take a break from the cosmopolitan scene of Istria. There is no better way of experiencing this town than to walk around the Old Town, which is packed with astonishing buildings and traditional restaurants.

This historic area still displays the ancient Roman traces. For example, the main streets of Decumanus and Cardo Maximus are still kept in their original shapes. There is also a Roman square with two ancient temples. One of them was built in the 1st century AD, and is devoted to the Roman god Neptune.

If you feel the need to see more attractions, you will want to visit the Cathedral Basilica of the Assumption of Mary. This imposing structure is one of the most important historical sites in the region, and it was reconstructed in the 6th century under the Byzantine rule. Porec also has numerous Romanesque and baroque buildings, and well preserved Venetian Gothic palaces.

With its exquisite architectural gems, ideal Mediterranean climate, and a magnificent seaside view, it is hard not to be captivated by Porec. While this quaint town is certainly not the best place for a quiet getaway, it is very attractive and tourist oriented, with a wide range of restaurants, hotels, and shops.

The town is perfect for hiking, cycling and kayaking, and there are several boat excursions for those wanting to explore this stretch of coastline. The Brulo Beach, and Plava Laguna Beach are the nicest beaches in Porec, however visitors will also find other beautiful places to swim. Visiting this appealing destination and surrounding landscape will provide a unique and memorable experience. Porec is well connected to major cities such as Rijeka and Zagreb by bus, while the nearest airport is located in Pula.

Rovinj

Ever since the early 20th century, Rovinj has been renowned as one of the most visited tourist destinations in the country.

This stunning coastal gem is situated on the western coast of the Istrian peninsula, so it is well placed for daytrips to Porec and Pula, both less than an hour's drive away. Both places are full of great attractions, but Pula, because it's larger, has more to offer.

Like the rest of the region, Rovinj buzzes with tourists from April to October. Loaded with charm, amazing restaurants, and spectacular beaches, Rovinj makes a great place to stay overnight.

The town's biggest attraction is the Church of St. Euphemia, a Baroque church situated in the heart of the old town. The remains of St. Euphemia, the patron-saint of Rovinj, are kept in a Roman sarcophagus from the 6th century, while the church also has several paintings and works of art, including Gothic statues from the 15th century. The church also boasts a spectacular view from the bell tower, and when the weather is nice you can even see the Alps.

In Rovinj, there is so much wonder and beauty to see and explore. For a tourist craving a unique travel experience, Rovinj is the best destination. I would recommend that you spend most of your time in Rovinj visiting the old town, and the church, which remains the town's finest attraction, and exploring the picturesque narrow streets that surround it.

Near this beautiful town lies Monkodonja. The fort of Monkodonja is one of the biggest attractions in Rovinj. It is considered that Monkodonja had certain connections with the Greek city Mycenae, as remnants of Mycenaean pottery have been discovered in this area. Take a couple of hours to wander through this mystical area.

For a glimpse of how the locals lived many centuries ago, when Rovinj was a Roman settlement called Arupinium, visit

73

the small but very revealing Native Museum of Rovinj. Housed in the baroque palace of Count Califfi, the museum displays several interesting collections, including the splendid ethnographic collection of folk costumes, tools and other artifacts, as well as some truly intriguing archeological finds.

If you get tired of sightseeing, you could visit the Forest Park Golden Cape. Many visitors come here just to stroll leisurely through the park, but there are many opportunities to enjoy nature. It is a hauntingly calming place with a wide variety of plants, inviting bays, rocky capes, stunning beaches, and well-organized walking trails. The park is also known as Punta Corrente, and is situated in the southern part of Rovinj, next to the Hotel Eden. As you can see, Rovinj is the epitome of a picturesque Croatian town.

Chapter 11: Slavonia - The other side of Croatia

Slavonia is one of the smaller regions in Croatia, stretching over the Sava and Drava rivers to the Hungarian border. This fertile region is a mostly rural area of bare rolling hills, plains, and green pastures. Dotted with numerous meadows, fields, forests, lakes, rivers, vineyards, historic castles, and a few bustling cities, the region features both diversity and serenity.

Kutjevo

If you are a wine lover, Slavonia is the best place you could ever visit. The region is home to some of the country's nicest wines, many of which are produced at the famous Kutjevo Vineyards. Although not a major tourist destination, the town of Kutjevo can cater well to any tourist with dozens of hotels, shops, and restaurants. There aren't many regular tourist attractions, but the town is a maze of narrow streets, beautiful buildings, and pretty squares where you can find plenty of small and affordable dining establishments serving some traditional local delicacies. Kutjevo Vineyards also offer lodgings for overnight stays as well as several restaurants, while the town itself boasts some of the most fascinating and dramatic countryside in Slavonia.

While in Kutjevo, plan a day-trip to the Papuk Geopark, which is a great place to unwind. Widely regarded as one of the most beautiful nature parks in Croatia, Papuk is well known for its fertile, green fields, massive hills, and beautiful forests. Still undiscovered by most tourists, Papuk is less crowded and not as frequently visited as other parks in Croatia. The area is home to the endangered brown trout, numerous plant species, caves, and archaeological sites. This is a great location to engage in innumerable activities, such as horseback riding, climbing, paragliding, geocaching, and mountain biking.

Vukovar

It is important to mention that this beautiful region experienced more damage than any other region in the country. The shelling of Vukovar is one of the most horrible events in Croatia's history. Vukovar, the Hero Town, situated at the confluence of the Vuka River and the Danube, was completely destroyed in the 1990's. During the Croatian War of Independence, Vukovar was overrun by the Serbian forces and thousands of people were massacred, numerous went missing and 22,000 civilians were forced into exile. The fall of Vukovar came as a shock to the entire world, because the city experienced one of the worst massacres in Europe since World War II.

Ever since, thousands of people from all over the country, and Bosnia and Herzegovina gather in Vukovar each year to commemorate the victims who were killed during the war. Today, some parts of the city are still destroyed or damaged. One of the most well known symbols of the Homeland war is the water tower in Vukovar. This legendary structure was heavily attacked more than 600 times during the war. Vukovar also has a museum dedicated to the siege.

Despite all the historic tragedies that have played out here, the region has many beautiful places worth exploring. A number of castles and old forts are scattered throughout the region. Two of particular interests are the ruins of the old forts Kaptol and Velika. The first one was built in a late gothic-renaissance style but the fort's actual construction date is unknown. In Velika, on the southern edge of the Lapjak hill, lies another fort known as Fort Velika. It was constructed in the 13th century and is definitely worth visiting. While many visitors skip Slavonija altogether, the region has decent museums, beautiful towns, quality local wines, and there is always plenty to see and experience.

Osijek

Osijek is the fourth largest city in the country and in recent years has emerged as a favorite travel destination. Osijek is also the biggest city and the economic and cultural hub of Slavonia, as well as the administrative centre of Osijek-Baranja County. Coming here is an easy day trip from Zagreb, or you may want to combine a visit with an overnight trip to Kutjevo or Kopacki Rit.

Crammed with hotels, restaurants, and plenty to do day and night, Osijek is a great base for exploring Slavonia's hidden attractions. Reaching this region is relatively easy too since is well connected to the rest of the country.

Osijek is situated on the bank of the Drava River, and evokes its rich history with pride. Many years before it began to sparkle in its current glow, the city was under the rule of the Austro-Hungarian Empire. Also, Osijek was one of the most severely damaged cities in the Croatian War of Independence.

Getting around Osijek is easy and a car is not necessary. You can travel around the city and several nearby settlements on foot, or by taxi or bus. The main attraction in Osijek is Tvrda, the oldest part of town. It is the best-preserved and biggest set of Baroque buildings in the country. In the Middle Ages this legendary site was the center of medieval Osijek, until the Habsburgs transformed it into a fortress. It was built on the bank of the River Drava, where it still stands today. Although some gates and bastions are missing, this magnificent fort still retains its medieval charm, and is well worth visiting. For a leisurely walk through the area, give yourself about 30 minutes.

Osijek's rich history is very much evident in its buildings and landmarks. While exploring Tvrda, you could visit the Church of St. Michael the Archangel. Built in 1742, the church does not fail to impress with its large bell towers, and beautifully decorated baroque pulpit. The church was actually built by

Jesuits, on the remains of Kasimpasha mosque. During the Homeland war the building was destroyed, but it was subsequently restored.

Also worth visiting is the Upper Town, which is known for the Parish Church of St. Peter and St. Paul. Famous for its large spire, it is the tallest structure in the country outside the capital city of Zagreb. It was built between 1894 and 1898, with frescoes made by the famous Croatian painter Mirko Racki. This beautiful church was built on the orders of Bishop Josip Juraj Strossmayer, who left a huge impact in our history.

Another architectural jewel is the Church of St. Michael the Archangel. Built in 1742, its baroque appeal is similar with the aforementioned Tvrda. The church features two frontal bell towers, custard-colored facade and various windows, which is not common for Croatian sacral architecture. An interesting fact regarding this structure is that it was built by Jesuits.

However, Osijek has a lot more to offer. If you would like to spend some peaceful time in nature, you can find several gardens and parks all over the city. One of the best ways to truly experience this city is to visit the legendary Pedestrian Suspension Bridge over the Drava River. It is a favorite gathering place for many locals, and features a great view of the city.

Kopački Rit Nature Park

If you really want to experience this region, then you have to visit Kopacki Rit Nature Park. It is a zoological and botanical reserve located close to Osijek, and is one of the biggest and best preserved wetlands in Europe. Since its designation as a nature reserve in 1976, Kopacki Rit Nature Park has been a cherished part of the region's rich offerings. It is easy to see why. You are bound to see the best of nature wherever you go.

Kopacki Rit Nature Park has served for decades as a sort of living natural museum. With 177 square kilometres of sprawling wilderness to explore, Kopacki Rit stands as one of Slavonia's biggest assets. Large herds of deer are basically the main symbol of this amazing park. There are other animals in the park, including wild cat, and pine marten. Also, Kopacki Rit's wet and varied terrain makes it a paradise for those who enjoy bird watching. Currently, there are over 300 different bird species. The park's immense network of tracks will take you to hundreds of unspoiled places, but the easiest way to explore the park is on excursion boats. This wonderful place is open year-round for visitors to enjoy.

Chapter 12: Jewels of the Adriatic just waiting to be discovered

It is next to impossible to explore all the beautiful islands in Croatia, so you will have to decide early which one is for you. But with so many great Croatian islands that you can visit, how do you choose the best island for you? That is a hard question that many tourists deal with. I have some suggestions and can give you some great overviews that will help you decide.

Korcula

Situated just off the Pelješac peninsula in Dalmatia, Korcula is the second most populous island in the country. It is also one of the prettiest islands in Croatia, covered for its greater part in woodlands and vineyards. Unfortunately for Korčula, its proximity to Dubrovnik, Hvar, and Split means it is often overlooked as a sightseeing destination.

The island is famous for its medieval towers, beautiful beaches and stunning harbor. Also, it's a pleasant place for nature lovers, and its old town is remarkably easy to get around. As the sixth-largest Adriatic island, Korcula draws tourists year-round, but it is particularly crowded in the warm summer months when the beaches are jam-packed. The Vela Przina beach is the biggest and most popular beach on the island, while Bilin Zal is one of the most beautiful beaches in Croatia. Korcula is linked to major cities by a regular ferry and bus services, so it's easily accessible, too.

This verdant and fertile island, cooled by the Adriatic Sea breeze lacks the general bustle of Croatia's other islands, and is perhaps the quintessential Croatia that most travelers imagine. The town of Korcula is the heart of the island, and it is best explored on foot. It has a charming, soothing vibe that is hard to feel in the country's better-known destinations. The town of Korcula was the birthplace of Marco Polo, so Korcula even has its own Marco Polo museum.

The tower of St. Mark's Cathedral beautifully dominates the scenic skyline of this picturesque town. The Cathedral was built in the 15th century, and houses works by renowned local and international masters, including several sculptures by Ivan Meštrovic, Croatia's most notable sculptor.

After exploring Korcula, find the time to also explore the quaint village of Lumbarda, which is renowned for the quality of its white wines and beautiful sandy beaches. This charming village is not only famous for its attractive appearance, but also for its rich culture and heritage. Numerous festivals and cultural programs in Lumbarda are held in the summer months, so you will certainly find something that will satisfy your preferences. This charming village is situated on the eastern side of the island, approximately 6 kilometers away from the town of Korcula, so you can easily reach it on foot.

Lastovo

Sometimes a place becomes known simply for its beauty and nature. Lastovo is such a place. The island of Lastovo is located approximately 20 kilometers from Korcula, and is very well connected by Jadrolinija ferry service with Dubrovnik, Split, and Korcula. Lastovo and its archipelago are a nature park since 2006, and consist of 46 islands and islets, with a wide range of flora and fauna. Lastovo is an ideal choice for visitors in search of tranquility.

Lastovo is the biggest town on the island, and there you can enjoy the nearby attractions in a climate which is nearly perfect all year round. The finest architectural gem of Lastovo is the Church of Saints Cosmas and Damian. It is located in the oldest section of the square in the town of Lastovo and dates from the 14th century. On the southern side of Lastovo you can find the Church of Saint Mary from the 14th century, which is the most visually appealing church on the island. The town also houses a number of buildings of great historical value from the 15th and 16th centuries.

The annual Poklad festival is the liveliest event on the island. It celebrates a tremendous victory of locals against Catalonian pirates in the 15th century. The Poklad takes place every February and is perhaps the greatest attraction for tourists.

Lastovo has a great selection of mostly uncrowded beaches, and some great tourist facilities. You can also find all kinds of entertainment especially those associated with the sea. Because this beautiful island is so isolated from more civilized areas, it boasts a completely different vibe that is immediately captivating. This is also one of the sunniest islands in the country, thus it caters to a sun-loving group of vacationers who appreciate its natural beauty and lack of formality.

Mljet

Mljet is one of the most appealing of all the Adriatic islands. Many of its scenic expanses are truly breathtaking. The National Park of Mljet occupies the western stretch of the island, Big Lake, Small Lake, Soline Bay and a large sea belt. The main parts of the park are Veliko jezero (Big Lake) with the Isle of Saint Mary, and Malo jezero (Small Lake).

The largest settlement on the island is Babino Polje, which is famous for its white washed houses. This small village is quite compact and made up of narrow streets and old houses. It is a charming place to stroll for an hour or two. This area has numerous breathtaking spots and a slower, more peaceful pace of life than Korčula Town or Krk Town.

Mljet has always been considered as an ideal holiday destination because it combines an excellent climate with an extraordinary landscape. As the greenest island in the country, Mljet has beautiful forests, interesting sights, rich cultural heritage and numerous atmospheric restaurants and tavernas. The most pleasant months to visit Mljet are generally April and May, or September and October.

This unspoiled island also played an important role in Odysseus's travels. It was a place of Apostle Paul's shipwreck. Mljet really is an explorer's haven in its exterior. In fact, one of the best things to do here is to rent a bike and discover this jewel at your own pace.

Mljet also boasts the oldest national park in the country and several caves, and it's definitely a must for anyone visiting this part of Croatia. Still, this gorgeous island is less touristy than Hvar and Korcula, and for that reason, it has only one hotel, the three-star Hotel Odisej. However, private apartments are also available. You can reach this incredibly alluring island by Jadrolinija ferry service from Dubrovnik, Korcula, Hvar, Split and Rijeka.

Lošinj

Everyone has a favorite Adriatic island, but it is perfectly clear why Lošinj draws visitors back again and again. Lošinj's flavors never fail to impress your senses. Situated in the Kvarner Gulf, the tiny island of Lošinj offers calm waters, picturesque fishing villages, great cuisine, superb climate, low prices, secluded beaches and no poisonous snakes. If you want to explore this beautiful island, or just want to rejuvenate, Lošinj is the place to go. It is no wonder Lošinj won a title of Croatia's Tourism Champion in 2007.

From Pula and Split, there are several options available for your transfer to Lošinj. The most popular is by seaplane. There is a small airport on the island, which offers a weekly flight to the island of Krk. From there, you need to take the ferry or rent a car. This long journey has many advantages. The island seems made for rejuvenation, relaxation and recharging. The lushness and beauty of Lošinj are truly admirable. Famous for its mild climate, and stunning vegetation, Lošinj blooms with palm trees, wild herbs, and spectacular plants. In addition, the island boasts a wide array of attractions that will compel you to stay for at least a day or two.

The main center of Lošinj is the town of Mali Lošinj, where you can find the highest concentration of hotels, konoba-inns, and restaurants. Tranquil and picturesque are just some of the normal descriptions that this charming town often gets from visitors.

Mali Lošinj boasts that enchanting Mediterranean appearance, and has a plethora of cultural landmarks as well as a very distinct architecture. In the evening the streets near the town centre are pleasant places of enjoyment where you can simply stroll around or have a drink. The town of Mali Lošinj is situated in the most protected part of the Lošinj bay, and while it doesn't offer much in terms of sightseeing, there are some beautiful churches, historic buildings, and fine beaches.

Cres

Blessed with year round mild weather, Cres is the biggest Adriatic island. It is situated in the northern half of the Gulf of Kvarner, while its southern side is well connected to Lošinj by a large bridge. Cres can be easily reached by a ferry from Krk, Rijeka, or from the Istrian peninsula. This beautiful place has a wild, untamed vibe that is refreshing and inviting. Although Cres is sparsely populated, its population doubles every summer.

The entire island is covered in dense primeval forests, and has a relatively large number of nonvenomous snakes. Cres is famous for its beautiful Lake Vrana, which is one of the deepest lakes in Europe. Thanks to its diverse landscapes, Cres is a great holiday destination with great hotels, beaches and gourmet experiences. Cres also has many villages worth exploring, and all of them are linked by a road that runs down the middle of the island.

Although the island has developed over the last few decades mainly as a family destination, numerous beaches around Cres never get crowded due to the large size of the island. Cres is well known for its unspoiled nature and dozens of small coves, bays, beaches and valleys.

Numerous villages around the island have become popular summer destinations thanks to their breathtaking beaches and emerald green waters. Cres Town in particular, with its narrow streets, splendid architecture, charming shops and pavement restaurants is a great base for those who want to escape from the bustle of the fast moving world. The main settlements around Cres Town are linked by well marked pedestrian trails, so you can indulge in long strolls.

Make sure to explore the splendid village of Lubenice. This picturesque place has a history of over four centuries, and is perched on top of a cliff. Apart from swimming, this small settlement is also great for hiking. Hiking trails cross the area and lead to many fantastic vistas and hidden corners.

Krk

Krk is everybody's favorite island. Situated in the northern Adriatic Sea, Krk is also the most populous island in the country. The Krk Bridge, which connects the island to the mainland, has the second longest concrete arch in the world. But you don't have to cross the bridge to reach Krk, since the airport Rijeka Krk is conveniently situated on the island.

A mountainous island of steep inclines, Krk is full of hidden surprises. One of them is the beach in the tiny village of Cizici. This inviting beach is well known for its healing mud that can actually help resolve the most common skin disorders. One of the most beautiful beaches in the country, at least in my opinion, Baška beach is also located on this stunning island.

Throughout its long history, Krk was desired for its geographical position, stunning landscapes and abundant natural resources, making the island a vital part of the Venetian Empire. Krk truly has an important role in our written history. Besides the nature, landscapes and beaches, it is the location where the Baška tablet was discovered.

Today, Krk has a cosmopolitan flair combined with a special traditional atmosphere. The island is packed with konobas, traditionally decorated dining establishments which offer local specialties. The variety of culinary experiences here is staggering. You could literally restaurant-hop from one town to another without ever leaving the island. Krk has numerous beautiful towns and villages worth exploring. The largest town on the island is called Krk. This ancient city is among the oldest settlements in the country. Roman remnants can still be seen today in some areas of the town.

At the same time, Krk also offers many hiking, cycling, surfing, sailing, and mountaineering opportunities. One of the best ways to spend a day is to take a boat tour and explore some of the finest beaches in Croatia. Whether you are looking for sandy beaches, unspoiled island nature or history and culture, Krk has it all.

Other important place is Malinska. It is a charming town on the northwestern part of the island, and one of the most visited tourist destinations in the country. Its attractiveness and mild climate make it an attractive place to live, which explains why so many people live here. The town has a lovely port, and a large number of shops, bars, and restaurants. In addition to shopping, the main activities here are sunbathing and swimming.

Pag

Pag is the fifth largest island in the country, and the one with the most extensive coastline. The island has two towns, Pag and Novalja, as well as many charming settlements and tourist hotspots.

Pag is famous for its crazy nightlife, wonderful beaches, delicious cheese, and of course, its unique lace. Pag lace, locally known as Paška Cipka is a unique handicraft produced only on the island of Pag. This intricate lace tells a story about the island, its origin, and rich heritage. The specificity of this traditional piece was recognized by the UNESCO's Representative List of the Intangible Cultural Heritage of Humanity. You won't be short of opportunities to find this splendid item throughout the region.

Also, there are so many wonderful dishes you must try when visiting Croatia, but if there is one thing you will eat over and over again during your visit - Paški sir. It is made from the sheep raised on the island of Pag, and you will be able to find it in every local restaurant.

Pag is also world famous thanks to its amazingly bustling nightlife, a good part of which is centered on Zrce beach. It's is easy to find pulsating nightlife and daytime partying on Zrce. However, anyone who visits Zrce will tell you it's far from normal. There are too many drunk people, and the prices for drinks and club entrance fees are mind-blowing. However, Zrce still attracts thousands of tourists, despite rampant promiscuity and high prices. There are several discotheques and wild bars in this part of Pag. If you want to party hard regardless, choose Novalja as your base. Zrce Beach is situated approximately 2 km from Novalja's center.

Luckily, the town of Pag also has more family-oriented beaches. Although this island is relatively dry, you won't have a hard time finding a great place under the sun. You can reach this beautiful place by bus from Zagreb or Zadar, and there is also a catamaran line between Pag and Rijeka. Overall, Pag is the best destination for young partygoers, but it is also amazingly family-friendly.

Chapter 13: Nature's playground - Croatia's most spectacular National Parks

Numerous National Parks in Croatia encompass the great diversity of natural beauty of the country, giving visitors a dose of everything from waterfalls to rivers, hills to soaring mountains. Croatia's National Parks feature some of the country's most amazing landscapes, natural formations and wildlife. From Plitvice Lakes, to the isolation of Paklenica National Park, here are some of the best national parks and nature reserves in Croatia that should be on your must-visit list.

Plitvice Lakes National Park

Plitvice Lakes National Park is certainly the most spectacular natural wonder in the country. In addition to the numerous waterfalls, a wide array of wildlife can be seen, including fish, frogs, brown bears, wolves and a range of bird species. If you have ever seen a charming picture with strikingly beautiful waterfalls flowing through lush forests, you have probably seen this oasis. The park was inscribed on the UNESCO World Heritage List, and should be included on your itinerary if you wish to see the best of Croatia.

You can reach this scenic place by bus from Zagreb, Zadar or Split, but your safest bet is to take a taxi. I recommend getting here the day before your tour. You can spend a night or two at one of their charming hotels or cottages. Accommodations are traditional, but it is well worth it to arrive here as early as possible to avoid the crowds.

The entire area is surrounded by verdant vegetation and wonderful sights can be found all around the park. This beautiful place is the best example of how Croatia has managed to preserve not only its rich cultural heritage, but also its natural beauty.

Plitvice Lakes National Park is one of the oldest national parks in this part of Europe, and features a series of waterfalls, 16 crystalline lakes and deposited travertine barriers. The two biggest lakes, Proščansko jezero and Kozjak jezero, are also the deepest lakes in the park. The highest and most incredible waterfalls are Veliki slap at the foot of the Lower Lakes, and Galovacki buk at the Upper Lakes.

Since its opening in 1949, this heavily forested national park has attracted legions of visitors to its scenic grounds. The main activities here are obviously hiking and walking, so make sure that you are fully prepared. The park, which encompasses over 295 square kilometres is well known for its idyllic setting. It is located right between the Mala Kapela Mountain and the Plješevica Mountain amidst the Dinaric Alps. With a multitude of serene landscapes, towering waterfalls, and a number of great hiking trails, the variety of beauty in this area will captivate even the most demanding traveler.

There are several trail options you may choose from, once here- they range in both difficulty and time. Some of them have water transfers available. In case you are planning to visit Plitvice, first decide during which season you plan to visit. If you don't like crowds, there are some secluded paths and areas to explore at your own pace. Entrance fees vary depending on season.

Northern Velebit National Park & Paklenica National Park

The Northern Velebit National Park covers a huge area of the northern section of the Velebit Mountain, and has innumerable trails, meadows, forests, and large summits with endless untouched scenery. Although the Northern Velebit National Park is the youngest national park in the country, it should be a necessary stop on the itinerary of every traveler to Croatia. We could say that this place has it all- numerous peaks, dizzying heights, abundant wildlife and fewer visitors than Plitvice lakes. The park received national park status in 1999, and has grown in popularity ever since.

The park comprises some of the most spectacular areas of the Velebit range, and is located within the Velebit Nature Reserve. It is home to many animals including bears, golden eagles, and wolves. The Northern Velebit National Park is the best place for outdoor enthusiasts, and is generally open from May until the end of November for wildlife viewing, sightseeing, and other popular activities.

In addition, there are numerous hiking trails and various cycling routes that lead towards impressive landscapes. Premuzic Trail, in particular, runs through the most diverse and beautiful sections of Northern Velebit. Elsewhere in the park are vast areas of unspoiled and often inaccessible scenic wilderness.

This green oasis offers numerous opportunities for those who want to combine relaxation with recreation. In fact, it would be much easier to name the things and activities that are not available. The village of Krasno seems made for long walks, while the Zavizan peak is the best starting point for mountaineering excursions. There are several mountain huts on Zavizan, but I would recommend staying in the adjacent towns and villages of Krasno, or Jablanac. The park also has a large nature reserve where one of the world's deepest caves was discovered in 1999.

The entire mountain massif of Velebit is actually a nature park where you can find some of Croatia's most idyllic landscapes. Paklenica National Park is situated on the southern side of Velebit Mountain. It is the country's second oldest national park, and one of the most well-known parks in Croatia. The park is located in Starigrad, near Zadar. You can easily reach this amazing place by bus from Zadar or Rijeka. The journey usually takes around 45 minutes, but it is well worth it.

Many people visit Paklenica National Park for the hiking and walking trails that cover the park. The top tourist attractions here are two canyons: Mala (Small) and Velika (Big) Paklenica. The park, with its rewarding sweeping views and panoramic vistas is a great place to take long walks. It has over 150 km of hiking trails and paths that are open to the public. The trails are well organized and marked with boards and signs for relatively easy exploration of this splendid location. In addition, the central area of the park also offers some truly spectacular panoramic views of the valleys nearby, while the massive peak of the Vaganski Vrh is the greatest symbol of this park.

To experience this vast and beautiful area on foot, you will need a good pair of hiking shoes. But Paklenica National Park isn't just a hiker's paradise. It is also strikingly versatile, featuring hundreds of unique cave formations, streams, meadows, and small waterfalls.

There are also many animal species within the park, including the brown bears, as well as the endangered bird species such as the golden eagles, goshawks and more. The park houses countless plant species, too. There are many reasons why Paklenica National Park is so special. It is the most popular climbing destination in the country, and the biggest in Southeast Europe. Today, the park features over 350 equipped and upgraded trails of various difficulty levels, allowing easy access to many viewpoints, and secluded areas. The park is best visited in early spring, or late fall, when temperatures are mild and pleasant. Hotel rooms and other accommodations can be found close to the park.

National Park Brijuni

If you are a nature lover, then you have to visit the Brijuni National Park. It is a surprisingly beautiful and vibrant archipelago of fourteen islands situated across the village of Fazana. First-time visitors are often awestruck by its scenic landscapes. This wonderful place can be easily reached by boat from the village of Fazana. The boating trip to the park generally takes only about 20 minutes.

With its stunning geology, abundant wildlife and great recreational opportunities, Brijuni National Park, is one of the crown jewels of Croatia's national park system. Combine this with the park's picturesque landscapes, numerous geological-paleontological sites, archaeological sites, and the Safari and Ethno Park, and you have the perfect holiday destination. Or if you are up for something more adventurous, explore the dinosaur's footprints. The islands boast over 200 traces of dinosaurs.

Another huge draw is the 1700 years old olive tree that still produces olives each year. In fact, there are over 600 indigenous and exotic plant species on park grounds.

 But this incredible environment isn't just there to be looked at; it is also the perfect place for sightseeing tours. You could visit the little-known but absolutely fantastic archeological sites within the park, including the Byzantine castrum, and the splendid St. Mary's Basilica.

The park's long history means you are spoilt for choice when it comes to sights and landmarks. As one of the most prestigious and exclusive places in the country, the islands were Josip Broz Tito's summer residence. There is even a museum dedicated to Tito with pictures, and objects of the former Yugoslav leader. Nowadays, this astonishing park is one of Croatia's most visited destinations.

A year-round location, this exceptional place is often crowded in the summer, and is well known for its luminous sunsets and numerous outdoor festivals, such as Histria Festival and Ulysses theatre. Swimming and underwater sightseeing are the most popular activities here, but there is really a wide variety of recreational experiences. Among everything else, you can play golf, badminton, tennis, or rent a bike and explore the park at your own pace. If you decide to visit Brijuni, make sure to bring your camera because you will certainly not regret visiting this captivating destination.

Risnjak National Park

Risnjak National Park is situated in Primorje-Gorski Kotar County, which is the most mountainous and densely forested part of Croatia. The park attracts thousands of tourists each year who enjoy its wonderful landscapes and the wealth of outdoor activities on offer. The park is known for fantastic hiking, fishing, climbing, and bicycling, not to mention being a mecca for wildlife watching.

 A range of walking opportunities are available to visitors of all ages, taking in pristine streams, magnificent rock formations, or lookouts offering absolutely delightful panoramic vistas. If you decide to visit this picturesque place, don't miss the Leska Educational path. It is a circular path 4.5 km long, which passes through areas of stunning vegetation and through many amazing landscapes.

Veliki Risnjak is the highest point in the park and the second highest in the region. With the majestic Snjeznik massif dominating the landscape and the light blue source of the river Kupa, nearly every corner of Risnjak has its own unique character. Snjeznik is located close to the ski resort of Platak, which is one of the most popular resorts for tour skiing in the country. To reach Platak from Snjeznik, you will need around an hour.

Quaint lodgings are scattered through the park, but the Risnjak National Park guest-house is the main location for accommodation in the area. The Josip Schlosser Klekovski mountain hut can be found right below Veliki Risnjak peak. As you can see, Risnjak is a wonderful destination for an outdoor experience in Croatia.

Chapter 14: A warm farewell from Croatia

Words may not be enough to really describe the sheer beauty of Croatia. When you get tired of hearing about how beautiful my country is, go find out for yourself. However, be warned – a vacation here might very well ruin your future vacations, as nothing else will seem beautiful after you have visited Croatia. With a wide array of dazzling attractions, bustling cities, and charming villages to look forward to, you are definitely going to enjoy every single bit of your visit to my country.

PS: PLEASE LEAVE YOUR REVIEW

If you reached this last page, probably this travel guide has given you some ideas about your stay in Croatia!

Would you be kind enough to leave a review for this book on Amazon? It will help other travelers to find their way through this beautiful country!

Many thanks and enjoy your trip!

The trademarks that are used are without any consent, and the publication of the trademark is without permission or backing by the trademark owner. All trademarks and brands within this book are for clarifying purposes only and are the owned by the owners themselves, not affiliated with this document

THE END

Made in the USA
Las Vegas, NV
13 July 2021